The American Institute of Family Relations
5287 Sunset Boulevard
Los Angeles, California 90027

All three authors are associated with the
Department of Psychiatry and Behavioral Science,
School of Medicine, State University of New
York at Stony Brook.

JULIA HEIMAN is currently a Senior Research Scientist
with Long Island Research Institute and Research
Instructor at Stony Brook. Dr. Heiman has published
a number of articles on male and female sexuality.

LESLIE LOPICCOLO is a Research Associate at Stony
Brook. Ms. LoPiccolo has several years of clinical
and research experience in the treatment of sexual problems.

JOSEPH LOPICCOLO is an Associate Professor of Psychiatry and
Behavioral Science. Dr. LoPiccolo has published numerous
professional articles based on his years of clinical research
in the areas of sexual function and dysfunction.

Becoming Orgasmic:
A Sexual Growth
Program for Women

JULIA HEIMAN
LESLIE LOPICCOLO
JOSEPH LOPICCOLO

A SPECTRUM BOOK

PRENTICE-HALL, INC., Englewood Cliffs, New Jersey

Library of Congress Cataloging in Publication Data

Heiman, Julia.
    Becoming orgasmic.

    (Self-management psychology series) (A Spectrum
Book)
    Bibliography: p.
    Includes index.
    1. Sex instruction for women.   2. Orgasm.
3. Sex (Psychology)   4. Women—Psychology.
I. LoPiccolo, Leslie, joint author.   II. LoPiccolo,
Joseph, joint author.   III. Title.
HQ46.H43   301.41 '8 '0564   76-25185
ISBN 0-13-072652-4
ISBN 0-13-072645-1 pbk.

© 1976 by Prentice-Hall, Inc., Englewood Cliffs, New Jersey

A Spectrum Book

10 9 8 7 6 5 4 3 2 1

Printed in the United States of America

Prentice-Hall International, Inc., *London*
Prentice-Hall of Australia Pty. Limited, *Sydney*
Prentice-Hall of Canada, Ltd., *Toronto*
Prentice-Hall of India Private Limited, *New Delhi*
Prentice-Hall of Japan, Inc., *Tokyo*
Prentice-Hall of Southeast Asia Pte. Ltd., *Singapore*

Contents

2

GETTING TO KNOW YOURSELF 18

The influence of early experiences on your attitudes
towards sex.   Your personal sex history.
Dealing with your feelings and concerns about your body.
Where you get standards for evaluating yourself physically.
Visual exploration of your genitals.
How to deal with negative feelings, as well as ways to
develop feelings about your genitals.

3

EXPLORATION BY TOUCH 40

Explore textures of entire body, looking for differences.
What to do if you feel uncomfortable.
Exercises to help you relax.
Ways to strengthen your vaginal muscles.

4

TOUCHING FOR PLEASURE:
DISCOVERY 54

What does giving yourself pleasure mean to you?
A new way to look at masturbation.
How to deal with negative feelings.
Exploring your body for feelings of pleasure.
Some ideas to try.
Putting pressure on yourself and the tendency to become a
spectator.

5

TOUCHING FOR PLEASURE:
FOCUSING   *63*

Continuing exploration through touch.
What may be difficult for you.
Ways to focus on and increase your pleasure—including
sensate focusing exercises, body work exercises.
Exploring erotic literature and fantasy and any concerns
you may have about their use.

6

GOING FURTHER   *85*

Some things to think about which may influence your
progress.   The importance of feeling good about yourself.
Dealing with conflicts about making changes.
The female sexual response cycle.
Fears about orgasm and "letting go."   Role-play orgasm.
Ways to increase arousal and trigger orgasm.

7

USING A VIBRATOR:
A LITTLE HELP FROM A FRIEND   *104*

A new way to look at using a vibrator.
Different kinds of vibrators and how to find the right one
for you.   Exploring your body with a vibrator.
Concerns you may have about the use of a vibrator to
enhance sexual growth.

8

SHARING SELF-DISCOVERY
WITH A PARTNER   *116*

Expectations and apprehensions about sharing your
progress with your partner.
Sharing self-pleasuring with your partner.
Concerns from the woman's point of view.
Concerns from the man's point of view.
Taking responsibility for your own sexuality—learning to
initiate and refuse sex.

9

PLEASURING EACH OTHER   *131*

Ways to avoid putting pressure on yourself and your
partner.
The importance of trust and communication in learning to
pleasure each other.
How to use verbal and non-verbal communication to learn
about each other's sexual preferences.
Ways to give each other encouragement and support.
Positions for pleasuring each other.
Enjoying non-intercourse forms of lovemaking.
Becoming less inhibited in front of your partner.
Dealing with negative feelings about male genitals.
Concerns about using a vibrator during lovemaking.
Feelings about using fantasy with a partner.

10

INTERCOURSE—ANOTHER FORM OF MUTUAL PLEASURE *157*

Feelings about intercourse and other forms of sexual
affection.
Seeing intercourse as part of, rather than the pinnacle of,
sexual expression.
Appreciation as a key to encouraging change.
Concerns about genital size.
The value of additional clitoral stimulation during
intercourse.
Advantages and disadvantages of different positions for
intercourse.

11

ENHANCEMENT *179*

Guidelines for enhancing your sexuality.
Techniques for oral-genital and anal lovemaking.
Aphrodisiacs.   Ways to delay ejaculation.
Aging and continued sexual growth.

12

WHAT NEXT? *192*

Alternatives to consider if you are still dissatisfied.
Locating a therapist.   Choosing the best one for you.

Acknowledgments

If the tone of this books is confident, it is because the program it describes has demonstrated its effectiveness with a great many different women over the past seven years. Many of the procedures this book describes were first developed by Joseph LoPiccolo at the University of Oregon in 1969. Of course, no therapy procedures is ever generated out of thin air. Several other therapists had previously done work that contributed much to this program. Most directly influential were the therapy procedures developed by Donald Hastings and Arnold Lazarus; Alfred Kinsey's data on female sexuality and the work of William Masters and Virginia Johnson provided much of the theoretical basis for this program.

During 1969–73, this program was used at the University of Oregon Psychology Clinic with generally good results. At Oregon a number of students and colleagues suggested refinements and modifications of the program. Especially important to the development of the program was W. Charles Lobitz, at the time a graduate student and now a respected colleague. Chuck added several important elements to the program, and was generally invaluable in its development. In 1972, articles on the basic procedures were co-authored by Joseph LoPiccolo and W. Charles Lobitz, and appeared in various professional journals.[1] Leslie LoPiccolo, then a graduate student, also became involved at that time and contributed to the further development of the program.

In 1974 a unique opportunity for further work in the area of sexual dysfunction arose. The Department of Psychiatry at the State University of New York at Stony Brook, under the direction of Stanley F. Yolles, created a clinical research program in human sexuality. At Stony Brook, Julia Heiman, already involved in research on female sexuality, joined the program and added her individual skills and abilities.

By 1975 it was clear that the program worked. Individual or couple sex therapy, however, was reaching only a small percentage of the women who could potentially benefit from a program such as ours. It became apparent that an easily understood self-help version of this program would be useful for those women who could benefit from such help without the need for formal therapy. Sharing personal reactions gained from women who had participated in the therapy program over the past several years seemed to be of particular importance. Ideas began to take form, and the result is this book.

Julia Heiman and Leslie LoPiccolo spent many hours writing and rewriting each section—it is truly a joint effort. Authorship was arbitrarily decided by a coin toss. Joseph LoPiccolo was invaluable as a consultant–reviewer and his recommendations were incorporated into the book. The art work was done by Leonard Preston, who was particularly interested in the challenge of conveying feelings through his drawings. We feel his drawings greatly enhance the book.

[1]See Bibliography.

Special thanks should be expressed to Carl Thoresen, editor of the Self-Management Psychology Series, for his helpful feedback; Lynne Lumsden of Spectrum Books for her enthusiasm and encouragement; and Toni Benedict and Ted Bohn, who were kept busy typing and proofreading for many months. Trish Morokoff and several other colleagues also provided valuable critical comments along the way.

The illustrations showing the male and female sexual response cycles are adapted from *Human Sexual Response* by William M. Masters and Virginia E. Johnson, 1966, with permission of Little, Brown and Company, Boston.

1

Getting Involved

Where are you at this particular time in your life? You may be single, married, separated, divorced, or widowed. You may have several children or none at all. You may or may not be in the midst of a sexual relationship with someone. You may be under 30, over 60, or somewhere in between. There might be many conflicts going on in your life right now, or things may be pretty satisfying.

No matter where you are right now, as you begin to look through this book you will probably have mixed feelings. Perhaps you are wondering if this really is for you. You may be worried about whether or not you will get everything you want from it. On the other hand, you may feel unsure about exactly what you do want for yourself sexually. You may feel enthusiastic—or very hesitant—about beginning. Perhaps you are tempted to find a magic formula for changing. One thing we are fairly certain of is that you probably feel you want something more for yourself. You want to grow and explore your potentials and you see the enhancement of your sexuality as part of this exploration.

That's why we decided to call this book *A Sexual Growth Program.* Specifically, this program is designed to help women who have not yet experienced or who have difficulty experiencing orgasm. We have gathered the contents from successfully treating, in sex therapy, numerous women with a variety of problems, fears, and potentials.

Orgasm is certainly a satisfying aspect of sexual growth. And yet, as you proceed through the following chapters, you will find that orgasms are not an isolated part of your sexuality. Orgasmic response depends on many things. Of course, it depends on sexual arousal, but feeling sexual can be influenced by your ability to feel comfortable with yourself, with your ideas about sex, and with your ideas about men and women. So growing sexually has a lot to do with general personal growth. This book offers you a framework for learning more about your sexual feelings, changing those *you* choose to change, and deciding how you want your sexuality to continue to develop and fit into the rest of your life.

Perhaps you've already read books and magazine articles on sexuality and you've tried to make changes. You may have even attempted certain ideas of your own that you thought would help.

Many women we've seen in sex therapy come to us feeling like failures because the sexual techniques they'd tried didn't work for them. Perhaps you've felt at times that if you could just do things *the right way,* you'd be orgasmic. It's natural to feel this way at times, to put more pressure on yourself . . . to try harder. Doing this makes orgasm practically impossible, though. Rather than looking forward to and enjoying sex, you may find yourself wanting to avoid it, or getting it over with as soon as possible. There may have been times that you've "faked" an orgasm in order to protect your self-image and your partner's opinion of you.

We hope that reading this book will help you take the pressure off yourself. We have tried to make this experience more than just a conglomeration of techniques. Sexual growth is not a series of steps or techniques towards a goal. It is a process that involves *all of you*. It involves your attitudes, thoughts and feelings as well as your body. Learning to become orgasmic or more readily orgasmic is only a part of the process of lifelong sexual development. However, it is likely that you have some specific concerns about changes you want to make. We'd like to share a couple of the more frequent questions women have at this point.

Will I ever have an orgasm? If you've never experienced orgasm, it's natural for you to worry that you may never have one. Everywhere, sex seems to be the subject of endless discussion, particularly in current magazines and books. In some ways this has been good, as it has stressed the importance of *mutually* satisfying sex for women as well as men. However, with all the emphasis on sex, many women feel pressured to be instantly, regularly, and even multiply orgasmic, in order to feel sexually adequate. As one woman in therapy said, "I used to go to parties and look at the other women. I would be sure that I was the only one there who couldn't have an orgasm." Actually, the fact that you may not have had an orgasm yet is not unusual. Currently, at least 25% of the cases seen in sex therapy involve a woman who has never experienced orgasm. An even greater number of cases involve women who are orgasmic but who experience difficulty reaching orgasm some of the time.

There may be many reasons why you haven't yet experienced (or rarely experience) orgasm. For instance, your family's religious and moral values may have strongly influenced your own attitudes about sex. Or your positive or negative feelings about yourself as a person and about yourself as a sexual being may be conflicting with your attempts to feel more sexually satisfied. Your feelings about your present or past relationships with men, both on emotional and sexual levels, are likely to be important. How comfortable you are with your body and how familiar you are with sexual responsiveness and techniques may also influence whether or not, and how often, you are orgasmic. And there are also other possibilities, many of which we will discuss in the following chapters. It is possible to deal with those attitudes and feelings which are making it hard for you to experience orgasm. You can learn those things about yourself and your sexuality which will make orgasm possible.

What will it mean to be orgasmic?   Change usually involves some uncertainty, and you may be concerned about what changes becoming orgasmic may make in your life. How will you feel about yourself?

Many women have concerns of this sort, and often they reflect mixed feelings about being a sexual woman. Movies and books usually present female sexuality in ways that are not very appealing for most of us to relate to. The message is often that the sexy woman is at best not worthy of respect and at worst evil and dangerous.

Also, as children, our parents, who serve as models in so many areas, often hide their own sexuality from us. (Do you remember being surprised at the thought that your parents had intercourse?) Unfortunately then, as women we often grow up with very few models for female sexuality whom we respect and desire to be like.

So it's not surprising that you may feel somewhat conflicted about wanting to change sexually. Most women share some of these feelings. Right now, it will be important for you to trust yourself enough to begin to explore who you are and where you want to grow sexually.

Will becoming orgasmic improve my relationships with men (or with my partner or husband)?   If your relationship is a good one, you will probably find that becoming orgasmic will give you a more complete sense of pleasure and satisfaction from sex. However, becoming more sexually responsive or orgasmic will probably not improve other serious conflicts in the relationship. Sometimes it's difficult to tell how much problems in the sexual area affect other problems that a couple has. One way to sort this out is to ask yourself, "If sex was no problem, would there still be other serious conflicts in our relationship?"

Also, try thinking about your reasons for wanting to become orgasmic. Do you want to learn to enjoy your body and its responses for *yourself* or for the pleasure it can give your partner? You stand a much better chance of reaching your personal goals if you are attempting to grow in order to please *yourself* first. Learning to understand and have some control over your body enables you to begin to enjoy sex for the things it can do for you. This involves taking responsibility for your own sexuality, something we will talk about in more depth later on.

GUIDELINES FOR USING THIS BOOK

This book was designed so that you could use it in the way that is best for you. The first part of the book (Chapters 2-7), deals with exercises and learning experiences you can do on your own. The second part (Chapters 8-11) deals with how to improve your sexual relationship with your partner if you currently have one or expect to at some later time. Each chapter builds on the information and exercises in the preceding chapters. For this reason it's best if you begin with Chapter 1 and progress through the chapters, trying each exercise in the order they are suggested. Some of the exercises are optional, and at certain points you will be able to skip ahead or go back to previous exercises so that you can progress in the way that is most meaningful to you. *If you are already orgasmic,* we suggest you still read through *all* the chapters and try the exercises. Changing old patterns, examining your attitudes and feelings, and having some new learning experiences is equally important for you. The material in the chapters will help you do this.

We've included lots of information about sex, particularly about female sexuality, as well as comments that other women have made, and common thoughts, fears, or experiences. Often we give you some questions to think about—questions which have been helpful to others. These are questions that we found are important to ask the women we have seen and are now seeing in sex therapy. We hope that they will help you get as much as possible out of each chapter. Doing the various exercises is important, but your personal reactions to the experiences are equally meaningful for your growth. After all, sexuality involves your thoughts and feelings as well as your body, and change comes from exploring new ways to think and feel as well as new things to do with your body.

Each exercise requires that you have some time to yourself, time when you can be assured of privacy and are free of any responsibilities (at least temporarily). A good idea is to set aside an hour or so for each exercise when you can be sure you will be undisturbed by business, children, friends, the phone, or your partner—if you have one. If you have children, you might want to take advantage of times when they are in school or in bed. Exchanging babysitting with a friend or neighbor on a regular basis has worked for some women. If you have a partner or spouse, ask his help in making these individual sessions possible.

Take your time and read each section through before doing the exercises described. Become familiar enough with what you will be doing that you don't have to keep referring to the book as you do a particular activity. Try and think about the questions at the end of the suggested activities while your reactions are fresh in your mind.

We suggest the amount of time you should spend on each exercise and also the number of times to try each during the week. You may find you need more or less time than we suggest. That's fine. What's important is to find a comfortable rate of progress for you. At the beginning, plan on around four to nine weeks for Chapters 2–7, and three to six weeks for Chapters 8–10. Try to have at least three individual sessions a week where you try the exercises in the book and practice what you've learned. You may find that illness or other unforeseen circumstances may interfere at times. That happens. Try, as much as you can, to keep up some sort of schedule for this program. This is important because of the nature of what you'll be learning and exploring. Each new experience builds on previous ones and makes learning easier. Also, at times you may be tempted to give in to the part of you which resists further change. You will find that having a schedule for progress gives you a little push to help overcome these natural fears about changeing. We've included a summary at the end of this book to give you an overview of the "flow" of the exercises throughout the book. Don't feel you have to follow this exactly. Feel free to adapt this framework to your own needs.

You are not "every woman." You are yourself. You will have your own unique process of sexual growth. Some of the exercises we describe may benefit you a great deal, others may initially sound simplistic and even silly. Laugh about them, but try them, too—we've seen women surprise themselves with unexpected discoveries.

We've mentioned that change is a bit scary because it means interrupting comfortable, predictable (although often unsatisfying) patterns and risking potential disappointment as well as potential satisfaction. Change is also irregular. If you have ever tried to change other areas of your life—by dieting, learning how to dance, learning how to talk in front of a group of people, teaching yourself to be better at ice skating, swimming, tennis, or whatever you have tried—you have probably found that improvement occurs with stops and starts. To prevent giving up during the difficult spots, it is important not to expect huge changes all at once. *Growth,* whether physical or emotional, is a series of small and uneven steps, so it's important to enjoy each small change, experience it fully, and resist the temptation to devalue the change and yourself by worrying about how much further you have to go. It's very important to acknowledge whatever gains you make and to take credit for them.

Finally, relax. Give yourself time. The exercises, questions, and learning experiences we've included in this book are not tests of your ability which you can either pass or fail. Rather, they give you a chance to learn about yourself in ways which can not only enrich the sensual-sexual aspect of your life, but other areas of your life as well.

Before you go on and actually begin the program, we'd like to strongly recommend that you have a gynecological exam, if you haven't already had one in the last six months. This type of exam (also called a "pelvic") should reveal certain physical problems which, if they are present, may be interfering with your enjoyment of sex. It is currently being recommended by most doctors that women have such a checkup every six months. This is important for your general health as well. At this time, a pap smear (a test for early detection of cervical cancer) is routinely done.

IF YOU HAVE A SEXUAL PARTNER . . .

Because a sexual relationship involves two people, the sexual responsiveness of your partner can influence your own responsiveness. If the male partner has difficulties getting or maintaining an erection, or ejaculates before the woman has sufficient time to get aroused, this can directly influence whether or not she is orgasmic. If this seems related to your sexual experiences together, you should consider getting some additional sex therapy in order to work on these problems (See Chapter 12). However, you can progress through the first part of this book (Chapters 2 to 7) on your own.

If this is not a problem, you are probably wondering about how to integrate the learning experiences you will be having on your own into your sexual relationship with your partner. There are a couple of ways that others have done this that we'd like to share with you. Both of you should think and talk about these alternatives and make a decision about which ones you feel would work for you.

First, a general way in which some couples have shared this growth experience together is for the male partner to read through and try some of the exercises on his own. For example, the exercises on body exploration, thinking about feelings and attitudes, and self-pleasuring could be done by him too. Often men are surprised to find that they have something to gain from such exploration.

Also, going through a process similar to what his partner is going through often enables a man to be more understanding and supportive of his partner. Some men, however, have trouble being sympathetic, since to them it doesn't seem difficult to have orgasms. Whether or not your partner makes an effort to understand your attempts to change, we would like to caution him not to interfere, not to be critical, and not to try to direct you himself. Some reassurance from him will make changes easier, but his help is not essential for you to make some progress on your own. Later when you do try and do sexual activities together, his cooperation will be vital.

In terms of your sexual activities together, one possibility is for you to continue having sex with your partner as you've done in the past, while you individually progress through the growth program. This usually works best for couples whose sex life is enjoyable for both of them, and where there are no real problems except for the woman's difficulty in experiencing orgasm. For some couples though, feelings of frustration and pressure to have orgasm have disrupted or replaced feelings of pleasure in sex. When this happens, one or both partners may find sex unpleasant, and try to avoid it or get it over with as soon as possible. These feelings are understandable. However, continuing unpleasant sexual activity while you are involved in learning to become orgasmic can interfere with your progress. This makes sense if you think about any new way of feeling or behaving. At these times, you need a chance to have lots of good, positive experiences, with no constant reminders of unpleasant old habits, in order to feel motivated and encouraged to keep changing.

Try to evaluate how the continuation of sexual activity with your partner will affect your ability to make progress sexually through this growth program. Ask yourself about the quality of your sexual experiences together. Are they mostly positive and enjoyable or are they negative and unpleasant for you? Will you feel pressured to have an orgasm or to give your partner an orgasm during love-making sessions? Are you tempted to continue sex with your partner because you're worried about how he would feel about not having sex (including intercourse) for a while?

Both of you need to consider your feelings about this latter possibility. Discontinuing old sexual patterns which have been harmful or unpleasant in the past is the second alternative which has worked for some couples. In most sex therapy clinics, couples are usually asked to refrain from intercourse for awhile so that new sexual attitudes and experiences can be explored. "Banning" sexual activities such as intercourse does not have to mean you will be doing nothing physical with your partner. Rather, through a series of sensual massage experiences, you can begin to rediscover the enjoyment of sexual expression or feelings, without pressure to have intercourse. We shall describe the kinds of sensual activities that you can do a little later in this chapter. For now, we would just like you to consider this as a possibility.

Leaving intercourse out of sex can be a new experience. For many couples, making love has always meant intercourse and, at least for the male, orgasm. Not expecting or demanding this allows you to explore a fuller range of sensual pleasures which can become neglected in the "rush" to go on to intercourse and orgasm. This pattern can be destructive to your sexual enjoyment because you become focused on where you are going rather than on the pleasure of each moment. It's not surprising that couples who have been in a sexual relationship more than a couple of years often complain that sex between them was better earlier in their relationship. The fact that some of the novelty may have worn off is usually only part of the difference. There is also a tendency for couples to stop doing some of the enjoyable sexual things they used to do together. Many couples in the beginning of their relationship spend more time on sexual play than on intercourse. Once married, where "real" sex is okay, making love can easily become a pattern of hurried foreplay, quick intercourse, and ejaculation. The pleasures of touching, kissing, caressing, and fondling each other somehow get forgotten. Restricting or refraining from intercourse is one way to allow yourselves time to rediscover each other through the sensual experiences.

Yet the idea of not having intercourse, or of not having your male partner have an orgasm in your sexual activities together, may seem impossible right now. The difficulties most couples run into are trying to deal with the man's feelings of sexual frustration and the woman's feelings of guilt. Over time, many women who are seldom or never orgasmic find that they do enjoy feeling close and participating in their partner's pleasure during intercourse. By not having intercourse, you may feel badly about not giving in this way, especially for several weeks. Think about your own feelings and talk it over with your partner to find out his feelings and attitudes. During your sensual experiences together, we stress the importance of not trying to get sexually aroused. At times, however, your partner may become aroused, want to go on to intercourse, and find it frustrating not to be able to do so.

There are several things you can do if this situation occurs. Some men are able to adjust to the idea of no intercourse because they know that it's temporary and because they understand that in the long run it will be the most beneficial way for their partner to make her own sexual progress and for their sexual life together to improve. Other men find that they feel less frustrated if they have a physical outlet such as masturbation. Since couples often have conflicting feelings about masturbation, we'd like to spend a few minutes talking about it. Although much of the discussion applies to both partners, for now we are concentrating on the male, since in later chapters we will discuss further issues related to women.

Almost all males and a majority of females masturbate at

some time during their lives. Typically, males masturbate more frequently during their teens and prior to marriage, but a fairly large percentage of men continue to masturbate after marriage. Although we are all familiar with the tales of the ill effects of masturbation, we now know that masturbation is a normal and healthy pattern of sexual expression. In fact, research has shown masturbation to be beneficial to adequate sexual functioning, especially among women (more on this later). Unfortunately, most men and women grow up feeling very guilty about the fact that they masturbate. It was something that was hidden from parents and usually from friends too, for fear that it would be punished or ridiculed by others. If you, and here we are speaking to the male partner, still have some negative feelings about masturbation, it is not surprising. Or if you have been masturbating and don't feel badly about it, but find it difficult to mention to your partner, that's not unusual either. Sharing your feelings about the idea of masturbation will be something that may be easier to do after you finish this chapter, since we will give you a framework of ideas to think over. For now, what we are most interested in having you consider are the *benefits* of masturbation for you while your partner is progressing through her own sexual learning experiences.

1. The freedom to masturbate when you feel the desire to will allow you to enjoy your pleasuring sessions with your partner without feeling physically frustrated and emotionally resentful.

2. Your willingness to find some sexual pleasure and release by masturbating will tend to take an enormous amount of pressure off your partner. She will not have to feel guilty about not having intercourse, since you are trying to cooperate in making her chances of making changes easier. If you want to help her change, it is only going to be possible if you take a share in reducing any pressures she feels. Worries about pleasing you will keep your partner from focusing on and really enjoying her own pleasurable feelings. Being able to do this is crucial for a woman who is learning to become orgasmic.

3. Not having to focus on arousal and orgasm takes pressure off you also. Rather than trying to "give" your partner an orgasm

and have one yourself, you are free simply to enjoy what you're feeling. We suspect that you will learn some new information about your sexuality too. We have seen many men surprise themselves in learning that a sensual experience without intercourse or orgasm can be very satisfying and enjoyable.

Sometimes one person interprets a partner's masturbation as a rejection or as an indication that their sexual relationship is a failure. If you, the woman, feel this way, it will make it hard for you to help your partner deal with his sexual needs and feelings. You may tend to give a mixed message to your partner: He should not have to feel frustrated by not having intercourse, but at the same time, you are leaving him no alternatives for physical pleasure. In trying to work out this conflict, it will be important for you to talk over your own feelings with your partner. In turn, he could make an effort to reassure you that masturbating is a positive expression of his sexuality, rather than a negative reflection on your relationship. How do you both feel about this? You both may have to rethink some of your own attitudes about different patterns of sexuality. Whatever you work out, keep in mind that a solution should maximize the satisfaction and freedom to learn new patterns for both of you. That will probably involve some compromises and understanding on both sides.

Remember, too, that the male partner does not *have* to masturbate, particulary if he doesn't want to, in order to decrease physical arousal. Instead he may be able to adjust temporarily to moments of sexual tension without frustration. We have seen this happen with other men who are able to accept the situation (since it is temporary) and who simultaneously derive a great deal of pleasure from their *sensual* experiences with their partners.

We have discussed two alternative patterns you might decide upon as you proceed.

1. Continue sexual experiences as before. This option should be chosen *only if* the sexual experiences are comfortable and pleasurable for *both* partners.

2. Discontinue intercourse temporarily, or any activity that is uncomfortable or unpleasant for either partner.

A third pattern combines the first two. In other words, if what you do together sexually is not unpleasant for either of you, but is generally enjoyable, you may choose to continue this during the first part (Chapters 2–7) of this growth program. That will involve anywhere from one to nine weeks or so. When you are ready to begin the part of the book which involves both of you, you should then refrain from intercourse and follow the sequence of exercises described in Chapters 8–10. You will also be able to include some of the sensual massage experiences.

An important consideration when including intercourse in your sexual experiences together is whether or not to use a contraceptive. This, of course, is a personal decision, one which should take into account your feelings, as well as current medical knowledge about the effectiveness and the potential dangers of the different forms of contraception (See *Our Bodies Our Selves* in the Bibliography).

If you don't use contraception, there is a possibility that fears of pregnancy can interfere with your enjoyment of sex. If you feel this may be true for you, you may want to reevaluate your feelings about contraception, unless strong personal or religious beliefs prevent you from considering contraception. If you do use contraception, it is best to use a method which you feel comfortable with and which best meets your physical needs.

SENSUAL MASSAGE

Both of you are probably missing a lot of good feelings that different parts of your body can provide for you. The massage exercises we describe are called "sensual" because they encourage you to appreciate more than just sexual or genital feelings. There is no real line between sensual and sexual of course, but what we would like you to attune yourselves to are feelings other than genital feelings and mutually pleasurable activities other than sexual activities such as intercourse or oral-genital sex. We are not going to go into any detail on elaborate massage techniques. We have listed, in the Bibliography, some massage books that our couples in sex therapy have liked. What we want to outline for you are some general principles of a sensuous massage and some specific hints to help you experience as much satisfaction as possible. Feel free to expand on whatever you learn here.

1. First, set a mood for your massage. You can make the atmosphere as relaxed or romantic as is agreeable to each of you. Make sure the room temperature is comfortable for being nude together, and that the light is not too glaring—candles or dim light are especially nice. Put on relaxing music if you like.

2. Choose a time of the day when you both can have some privacy and uninterrupted time together (30 minutes to one hour if possible). You may want to do this just before you go to sleep; but watch out for fatigue—it can make you edgy, and decrease your ability to enjoy this experience.

3. Try to spend a little time together before you begin. You may want to talk or share a glass of wine. Or try sharing a shower or bath together first.

4. The main purpose of this experience is to increase your pleasure and awareness of your partner's response to physical— but not necessarily genital—kinds of stimulation. You will be taking turns caressing, stroking, and rubbing different areas of each other's bodies. Although you may find yourself becoming aroused, this is not the goal and you shouldn't *try* for arousal. The first few times you do this, we would like you to massage any areas *except* the genitals and the woman's breasts. Explore the toes, feet, thighs, tummy, arms, face, hair, and buttocks. Do this *slowly*—allow at least 10–15 minutes for each of you. Remember, this is not a gym massage. It is supposed to be sensuous, not a rub down, so try light brush touches as well as strong kneading touches. Use your palms, finger tips, finger nails, pieces of material, fur, your lips or hair.

5. As you are taking turns, it's important to *talk to each other* about what feels good and what doesn't. The person being massaged should try saying things like "good, harder, easy, use your nails more, go slower, mmm"—or, "yes, that's great" fairly often in order for the person massaging to be able to give the most pleasurable stimulation. The person massaging might say, "How's this?, or Does it feel better here?" if he or she is unsure about the other's feelings. It's *extremely important* to communicate your likes and dislikes in a good clear way. Communication allows you to give and receive pleasure in personal, more meaningful ways. Everyone has different needs and pleasures, and they change as the person changes. By letting each other know what feels good, you help make each massage (and later each sexual experience) less routine, more spontaneous, and more intimate.

6. On the third or fourth session together, you can include breast massage. Again, continue to explore different strokes and touches that each of you likes.

7. Gradually, by the sixth or seventh massage, or whenever you both feel pretty comfortable about it, add each other's genitals into your massaging. (You may want to wait until you are at Chapter 8.) Again, the idea is just to give yourselves pleasure, not to turn each other on. When it comes time to include genitals in massage, it is often tempting to zero in on that area and forget about the rest of the body. This can build anxiety and reduce the total pleasure of the experience. So when you do begin to explore the touching of genitals, try including them as just another source of pleasure and spend a proportionate amount of your massage time there.

8. While you are being massaged, try to focus on the feelings at the place where you are being touched: Let your attention remain on these feelings. If your thoughts wander, bring them back to your physical feelings and follow your partner's touch with your mind. This will help you get more pleasure and relaxation out of the massage. Remember, when it's your turn to be massaged, you have no responsibilities except to communicate what feels good and what would feel better.

9. If you find that your sensual massage sessions are not going well (or if they are and you just want to try something different), try changing the focus of your sessions. Instead of focusing on giving your partner pleasure, try massaging in ways which give *you* the most pleasure. The only restriction is that you do not do anything which is painful or in any way distressing to your partner. The partner who is being pleasured is to relax and focus in on his or her feelings rather than to guide or direct the massage. Often couples who were anxious or upset while focusing on their partner's pleasure are able to relax and enjoy massaging in this demand-free way.

All of the above suggestions have been useful for other couples. In addition, some couples like to try massaging with different lubricants (oil, lotion) in order to change the friction and texture of the massage. Oils tend to intensify the touches you experience, and make your skin feel warmer; lotions tend to be a bit sticky after they dry and make the skin feel cooler. Powder is another possibility, or any of the above in some perfumed fragrance is nice. Because the genitals are extremely sensitive, don't use anything on your fingers when massaging here except a sterile lubricating gel. "K–Y" or "Lubrifax" are such lubricants and are available over the counter in most drug stores. Explore and find out what's good for *you.*

Keep in mind that if you are in a bad mood, angry with your partner, very tired, or very distracted, it will influence how completely you are able to enjoy sensual massaging. Sometimes you will be able to overcome whatever is bothering you by letting the moment's enjoyment take over; at other times you won't be able to let what's bothering you slide. If you find that a sensual massage experience isn't pleasurable, or is making you feel badly, stop and try to discuss with your partner what is interfering. This gives you a chance to share feelings and begin to deal with the difficulty.

2

Getting to Know Yourself

Why is it that so many women have problems with sexual responsiveness? As we work with more and more women, we find ourselves puzzling over this question. No one really knows exactly why some women have no difficulty experiencing orgasm while others do, but we have developed a better understanding of some general factors that might be important. We'd like to talk briefly about them in the hope that some of the ideas may help you begin thinking about your own sexual development and putting your sexuality in perspective.

Certainly experiences we gather as we are growing up influence our feelings and attitudes about sex and our bodies. From the moment we are born, we begin to learn about our bodies. By the time we are adults, we have learned to recognize and have some control over hunger, pain, and fatigue; but often we may have very little knowledge, understanding, or control over our sexual functioning. Why? As children, we are usually encouraged to explore and experiment with what we can do with our bodies. We are encouraged in all sorts of ways to learn to use our bodies. For the very young child, for instance, learning might take the form of a "name game" where the parent names a part of the body and the child points to it. Success is usually followed by lots of attention and approval. Yet, in this fun and private learning context, the genitals are usually never mentioned. A child can interpret this omission in many ways: Perhaps the genitals are unimportant; perhaps they are too bad or dirty to talk about. Whatever the feelings the child gets, excluding the genitals as natural parts of the body can begin the process of isolating sexuality from the rest of a person's experience. Sometimes this message is much clearer. As recently as ten years ago, books on child rearing encouraged parents to ignore or distract their children when they were found playing with, touching, or fondling their genitals as this was thought to be harmful.

Most of us probably had learning experiences that suggested there was something different about "that" part of our body "down there." Most of us were not encouraged to recognize or explore our genitals, and certainly we were not encouraged to talk about or be proud of them. In fact, many women don't know exactly where their vagina is until after they have begun to menstruate (perhaps you remember trying to figure out how to insert a tampax from a diagram) or have intercourse. Similarly, the clitoris is kept "secret"—until recently most health books used in schools labeled the vagina but made no mention of the clitoris.

Your early experiences with menstruation can also influence your feelings about your body and your sexuality. Many young girls are totally unprepared, and understandably they find the experience of sudden bleeding a very traumatic one. For other women, their parents prepare them minimally, but with an attitude that menstruating is a "curse," dirty, or just a burden women have to bear. At best, having periods seems to be regarded as a bother more often than as a cause for celebration. Additionally, most of us learned very little information about sex when we learned about menstruation. Some basic information on why menstruation occurred and possibly a warning that "now you can become pregnant" may have been the extent of our introduction into sexuality.

With this learning history, it's not surprising that many of us grow up feeling less positive about our genitals and therefore with our sexuality than other parts of our body. For some women, the effect of these early experiences contributes to their lack of sexual responsiveness.

Whatever your background has been, it's very important to the kinds of attitudes and values you have about sex. How pleasant various experiences were for you helped to determine your feelings regarding your sexuality. Because your background includes certain features that no other person's does, we can't point out specific events that might have most strongly influenced you. We hope that you can begin to do this on your own by remembering situations that occurred with regard to your parents' attitudes toward sex and affection, in your first dating and sexual experiences, in any frightening sexual experiences, and in your relationships with men.

Thinking about some of the events in your life that have influenced your feelings and attitudes about things related to sex is a good place to begin this growth program. For this reason, we are including some questions which will help you get a picture of your own personal sex history. You may want to write your responses down so that you can refer to them again at some later time. If you have a partner, you may want to share some of your answers with him, or share some of your early experiences. However you choose to use these questions, we feel that they will prove helpful to you as a way to begin to put your experiences in perspective. Here are some suggestions for Exercise I—*A Personal Sex History:*

— Take your time on each question. In sex therapy we usually allow up to two hours or so for exploring these types of questions. You may want to think about some of them and come back to them later.

— Try to focus on each question as it relates to your feelings or attitudes about yourself sexually, or about sex in general.

EXERCISE I: A PERSONAL SEX HISTORY

RELIGIOUS INFLUENCES

1. Was religion an active factor in your early life? (Sunday school, parochial school, etc.)
2. In what ways did your religious upbringing influence your attitudes towards sex?

AS YOU WERE GROWING UP

1. Were you allowed to ask questions about or discuss sexual topics?
2. Was physical affection shown between your parents? How were your parents affectionate toward each other? (What behaviors do you recall?)
3. Were your parents verbally or physically affectionate with you?
4. What was the attitude toward nudity (or modesty) in your home?
5. What do you think your parents' attitudes toward sex were:
   a. With each other
   b. Toward your own developing sexuality
6. What influence did your siblings or friends have on what you thought about sex at this time?
   a. Was it ever discussed with friends or siblings?
   b. Was it the subject of jokes and embarrassment?
   c. Was it considered "dirty"?
7. Do you recall playing any games with sexual content as a child? (such as, "Doctor")

8. At what age do you recall first having pleasurable genital feelings?

9. At what age did you first experiment with masturbation (or any other solitary activity which produced genital feelings of pleasure)?

   a. How and where did you do this? How often?

   b. How did you feel about doing this?

   c. Were you ever discovered at this?

10. Do you remember any upsetting experience having to do with sex that occurred during your childhood?

11. When did you first learn about "where babies actually come from" and how they are conceived?

   a. How did you learn?

   b. How did you react to this?

12. At what age did you start to menstruate?

   a. Had menstruation been explained to you in advance? How and by whom?

   b. Was the subject discussed among your friends? What term(s) did you use to refer to it?

   c. What were your feelings in anticipation of menstruation?

   d. How did you feel after it had begun?

      1) Do you recall it influencing your life style in any way?

      2) Did you feel any differently about yourself and your body?

   e. Have you ever had any menstrual difficulties?

DATING

1. At what age did you start to date?

   a. In groups?

   b. On single dates?

PETTING

1. What kinds of petting did you engage in?

2. Where did petting behavior usually occur? Under what circumstances?

3. Was there any touching or manipulation of genitals involved?
4. How did you respond sexually to these behaviors?
5. How did you feel about engaging in these behaviors?
6. How would your parents have responded if they knew? What were their attitudes about petting or other non-genital sexual contact?

INTERCOURSE EXPERIENCES

1. Did you ever engage in premarital intercourse? If so, what was it like the first time?
2. When and where did intercourse usually occur?
3. How did you respond sexually? (Were you orgasmic? Did your partner have any problems with erection or premature ejaculation?)
4. Did your parents even discuss intercourse with you? Contraception?
5. What feelings usually accompanied intercourse?
6. Were you ever suspected or caught?
7. Have you ever had any problems with venereal diseases such as gonorrhea or syphilis?
8. What form of contraception do you use, if any? Whose responsibility is this? Any problems related to the type of contraception you're using?
9. Have you ever experienced pain during intercourse? Frequent vaginal infections?
10. Have you ever had difficulty achieving penetration? Is the penis unable to enter the vagina because of the tightness of the vaginal muscles?

OTHER EXPERIENCES

1. Did you ever have any sexual fantasies with masturbation, petting, or intercourse?
2. Do you remember any sexual encounters with a person of the same sex? If so, how did you feel about this?

3. Do you remember ever seeing a person expose himself or masturbate in public? How did you react?
4. Did you have any unpleasant experiences with undue physical intimacy with strangers or a family member or friend?
5. Do you remember any discussions about homosexuals? Or the possibility of assault or rape?

PREMARITAL BEHAVIOR WITH FUTURE SPOUSE

1. What were some of the different sexual behaviors you engaged in with your spouse before marriage?
2. Describe the quality of these sexual experiences. How did you respond sexually? Were you aroused, orgasmic, uncomfortable, tense or afraid?

CURRENT ATTITUDES AND BELIEFS

1. What is your attitude toward sex in general? What specific activities do you find enjoyable? Do you ever feel inhibited, embarrassed or guilty about any aspects of sex?
2. Do you feel positive/negative/or neutral about:
   a. Your genitals
   b. Masturbation
   c. Oral-genital sex
   d. Foreplay
   e. Intercourse
   f. Orgasms other than through intercourse
   g. Erotic literature
   h. Pornographic movies
   i. Sexual fantasy

You need not come to any conclusions by reflecting on your answers to these questions. It is basically a brief sketch of what may have been important influences along the way. And, what you have or have not experienced is less important than how you felt about the experiences. For example, if your parents were not affectionate toward you, did this bother you a great deal or did you just accept it? Whatever strong feelings you gathered in your childhood, adolescence, and early dating may still be with you and influencing how you feel about yourself, other people, relationships and sex.

As we mentioned earlier, there is no particular set of experiences that determines who will and who won't be orgasmic. There is not one "type" of woman who never or seldom has orgasms. However, there are several kinds of experiences that many women we see have in common. We will mention them briefly in order to give you an idea of how some experiences might influence sexual responsiveness.

Many women we have seen come from strict religious backgrounds, or from parents with very restrictive morals about sex. Sometimes this means that sex is regarded as dirty, that it is not to be discussed, and that it should only occur after marriage. Perhaps sexual thoughts and sexual activities might have been punished, or believed to be sinful. Because of this, many women just avoid doing anything sexual if they are strictly religious, or they are sexual but feel very tense while they are having sex and very guilty afterwards. Many of these feelings, of course, do not suddenly stop after someone marries. It's difficult to let yourself enjoy sex and be responsive if you have experienced years of feeling that it was not something "nice" women enjoyed. Other concerns that often accompany premarital sex, such as worries about being caught or becoming pregnant, are also likely to contribute to tension and to the lack of personal pleasure during sex.

For some women, sexual responsiveness is influenced more by the nature of their relationship with their partner and his sexual response. For instance, some women would like their mates to be more affectionate in non-sexual ways, but find it difficult to express this. An equally common problem is that many women would like more foreplay before intercourse and/or would like intercourse to last longer. Couples sometimes have difficulty talking about this also, and attempts to change sexual patterns often result in disagreements and hurt feelings, something we will discuss more in later chapters.

As you think your past and current experiences over, we would like you to keep several things in mind. One is that you are not born with certain feelings or a certain way or expressing yourself sexually; you learn these through a variety of experiences over time. That is what growth is all about, and that is why you can learn to develop new feelings and new ways to respond sexually. This brings up a second point: Even if you feel you know exactly why you have trouble sexually, *just knowing what's wrong is not necessarily going to make change occur.* It may help you understand who you are, provide you with some reassurance about yourself, and motivate you to do something about it; but changing is an active process. We have tried to make the exercises that follow meaningful ways for you to get away from old ideas and patterns of response and begin the process of exploring new dimensions of your sexuality.

EXERCISE II: LOOKING AT YOURSELF

PART I

As you've found in Exercise I, most of us have feelings and concerns about our bodies. These concerns often influence how we feel about ourselves in general and how we feel about ourselves sexually. This exercise will help you to become more aware of some of these feelings and will suggest some ways to deal with them.

For this exercise you should set aside 45 minutes to an hour when you can have privacy. There are two parts to this exercise which can be done separately or in one session. Try to clear your mind of other worries and responsibilities. This is your time.

Make sure, in some way, that the room you will be in is comfortable enough for you to be nude. We suggest you begin by taking a relaxing shower or bath. You will need a hand mirror, and if possible, a full length mirror.

While you are in the shower or bath, stop for a minute; just stand (or lie back) with your eyes closed and let the water run over your body. Let yourself relax. Now try to picture yourself in your mind. Can you see yourself? Open your eyes and look at your hands and arms, down at your breasts, stomach, legs, and feet. What do you see? How do you feel about what you see? Do you like what you see? How would you change what you see if you could? What you say to yourself may sound like this, for example. "I have nice arms. My hands look older, though. The skin is more wrinkled but they look like strong hands" and so on. After a few minutes, relax and finish your shower or bath. After you're dry, take some time (10–15 minutes or more) and look at yourself in a mirror (a large or full length one if possible). This may or may not be easy for you to do. Looking at ourselves with our eyes (as in the bath or shower) or with our mind's eye (as when you closed your eyes) is often easier than looking in a mirror. Often we see ourselves at those times in more accepting ways than we do in the harsh reflection of a mirror. You may find you've avoided looking at your whole body in a mirror, or that you've gotten into the habit of taking quick, fleeting glances from the most flattering angle. If so, you may want to keep your towel around you for a while. Give yourself time to relax and feel more comfortable.

When you're ready to begin, start at the top of your head: Look at your hair, the shape of your face, the texture of your skin, your eyes, nose, and ears. What do you see? What would you change if you could? How do these things make you feel about yourself sexually?

Next, move on to your torso. Remove your towel so you can become familiar with this part of your body. Look at your shoulders, arms, hands and fingers, breasts, waist, hips, pubic hair. Ask yourself again, what do I see? How do I feel about

what I see? What would I change? How do these things influence
how I feel about myself sexually? When you're done, go on to
your legs, feet, toes and ask yourself the same questions.

If you have a full length mirror, turn around and look at the
back of your body. You may want to try moving around a bit in
front of the mirror. After you feel you've spent enough time,
take a few minutes and think about this experience.

1. Was doing this a positive (pleasant) or negative (unpleasant) experience for you?

2. Were there parts of your body that influenced how you felt about yourself sexually? Were these strictly erotic or sexual parts of your body, like your breasts?

3. How do you stress the things about your body that you're proud of? How do you try to hide the things about your body you dislike?

4. What are the things you don't like about your body? Are these things *you* genuinely don't like or have you accepted the judgment or opinion of another person? If so, who are the people whose opinion of your body concerns you? Do they tend to be males or females?

5. Where did you get your ideas of what is attractive—your mother, men, yourself, T.V., magazines?

Most women feel dissatisfied with some part of their body. Sometimes these feelings are constructive, in that they prompt us to do something for ourselves that is important for our health. For example, losing weight or exercising if we are overweight or out of shape. Being overweight and out of shape or in poor condition *can* influence how free you feel to move and be active during sex, which of course influences how much you enjoy what you do. We have suggested some books in the Bibliography that other women have liked and found helpful in improving the condition of their bodies. If you found this experience unpleasant because you don't like the condition of your body, it will be important for you to work on changing this at some point in your life, for the sake of your general health as well as your sexuality.

Often, however, women don't like their bodies for reasons which they cannot and possibly should not try to change. Let's talk a little here about some frequent concerns women often have about their bodies.

Breasts: You may feel that your breasts are too large or too small. Perhaps you have suffered pangs of embarrassment about being the last one or the first one among your friends to develop. Padded bras, bust developers, exercisers, creams, and even surgical procedures have capitalized on and helped to maintain concerns about breast size. Actually, the size of your breasts is pretty much determined before your are born, just like your hair color, body build, and height. It doesn't reflect anything about you as a person and doesn't influence how sexually responsive you are; and it's not true that you must be buxom to be sexually appealing. At one time, large breasts were in vogue, but society's version of the ideal female form changes every few years. It was even the fashion not too long ago for women to flatten their breasts with tight corsets and cinches in order to look flat-chested. Since our culture's external standards of beauty are always changing, it will save you a lot of frustration if you can begin to accept and even appreciate your breast size for what it is.

Another variation among women is the amount of hair they have on their bodies. We all have some, since this is important protection for our skin and particularly the sensitive areas of our body. However, some women have only a little hair or light hair that is not very visible, while others have lots of dark hair that is far more visible. Many women have some hair surrounding the dark area (areola) of their nipples, and the amount of pubic hair a woman has around her genitals also varies. In some women, the pubic hair extends up from the genitals in a line up to or near the navel.

How you feel about this may be important. Whether or not you shave the hair off your legs and underarms, give careful consideration before you regularly remove hair from other areas of your body, since the skin may become irritated over time. For some reason, less body hair is considered more feminine in our culture. Yet a number of men consider a lot of hair around the pubic area to be sexually attractive. Also, the presence of hair often makes being caressed a more sensual experience. The amount, color, and texture of your body hair is part of you and is a normal variation among women just as it is among men. Like breast size, your body hair may influence how you feel about your appearance but it does not affect how responsive you are.

Often, women are inhibited about their bodies because they feel ashamed of any scars or stretch marks on their skin. Actually, such marks are quite common. Often, women have stretch marks around their hips and stomachs and their breasts whether or not they've had children. These are usually most noticeable to the woman herself.

Perhaps doing *Exercise II, Looking At Yourself,* has gotten you in touch with certain concerns you have about your physical appearance. You probably have others which we haven't mentioned here. If you feel these concerns are making it difficult for you to feel good about yourself sexually, you need to examine them carefully. We would encourage you to work on those things about yourself that you can change which are potentially dangerous to your health. But for those parts of you that you can't change, perhaps you need to do some rethinking about your standards for yourself. Pay particular attention to where your standards are coming from. The chances are very likely that your ideals have been adopted from T.V., magazines, and movies in which the stereotyped woman is large-breasted, slim, flawlessly complexioned, fashionably groomed, and barely 23. This image is as fictitious as an afternoon soap opera. If you feel pressured to be more perfect in order to please your sexual partner, remember that he too has been influenced by the same fabrication of what's "beautiful." Given the rather narrow definition of feminine beauty in our culture, it's a real challenge to learn to accept who you are and what you look like. We hope that being more aware of what influences your ideas of appearance will help you to begin to focus on your positive qualities, and not to let the things you don't like prevent your from feeling like you are a worthwhile person. But remember, too, that you don't have to be completely satisfied with yourself in order to grow sexually. As one woman who was halfway through our program said, "It's nice to know that even though my body's not perfect, it can still give me pleasure."

PART 2

How are you feeling now? If you feel like continuing, and you have another 15 minutes or so left to your hour, do so. If you feel rushed or tired or you would like a chance to reflect some more on the first part of this exercise, then stop for now and do this next time.

If you have decided to continue, take a few minutes to relax yourself. You may want to just lie down for a few minutes with your eyes closed. Or you may want to try controlling your breathing as a way to help you relax. If you want, try this now:

Lie down. Inhale through your nose slowly to the count of five. Feel your chest and abdomen expand and fill with air. Then, part your lips and exhale completely, pushing all the air from your lungs. Try this a few times with your hand on your stomach so that you can feel the air filling and leaving your body. Or, you may want to slowly raise your arms from the side (not in front of you) over your head as you inhale and lower them as you exhale. This will help your chest expand fully.

When you feel relaxed, prop your back against something such as a wall, a headboard, or several pillows. Using a hand mirror, we'd like you to look at your genitals. We've included a drawing to help you identify the different parts of your genital area. Don't worry if you don't look exactly like the drawings we've included. Genital appearance, like facial appearance, varies tremendously among women.

Begin with the bone and mound of hair which covers your genitals. This is called the *mons.* Feel the curved bone of the mons through your *pubic hair.* This hair serves to protect this very sensitive area of your body from irritation from clothes and perspiration. Your pubic hair may be thick or sparse and its texture and color will also be uniquely your own. Now move your fingers down the center of your *outer lips* or *labia majora,* which are also covered with pubic hair. These lips help protect the *inner lips* or *labia minora.*

Find your inner lips. These may be large or small. In some women they are completely hidden by the labia majora. In other women these inner lips are more prominent and hang down between the labia majora. These variations are normal. The color and texture of the inner lips will also vary. Yours may be basically pink or shade more towards the browns. The inner lips usually meet at the top of the *clitoral shaft,* although in some women they do not. Find your clitoral shaft. At the top of the

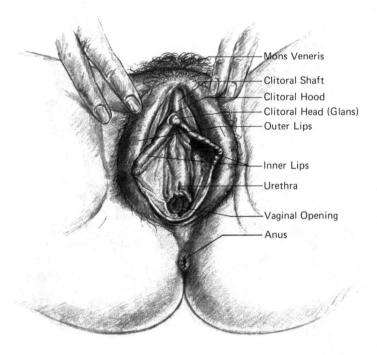

shaft is the *clitoral hood* and the *clitoris.* The clitoral hood is a fold of skin which covers a small round organ—the clitoris. The hood helps protect the clitoris, which is extremely sensitive, much as a foreskin protects the penis in a man who is uncircumcized. Pull back the clitoral hood and look at your clitoris. In some women, the clitoris seems to adhere to the hood so that the hood cannot be pulled back very much. This does not seem to be related to sexual responsiveness, and it is not necessary to surgically de-

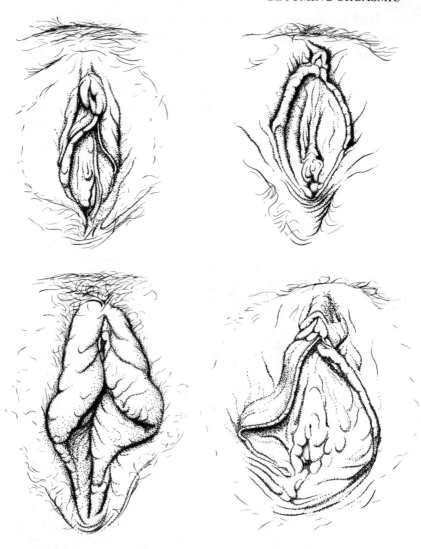

tach the hood. The size of the clitoris and its distance from the vagina varies from woman to woman. The clitoris is extremely sensitive to sexual stimulation. Years ago, it was thought that the vagina provided the main source of sexual stimulation for women. Today we know that although the whole body contributes to sexual stimulation, the clitoris is the most important source of sexual pleasure for women.

When you looked at your labia minora or inner lips, did you notice whether they are connected to the clitoral hood? If they are, during intercourse, the movement of the penis in the vagina will cause these inner lips to move. This causes the skin surrounding the clitoris to move and stimulate the clitoris. If the inner lips are not connected to the clitoral hood, it is possible for clitoral stimulation to come from direct contact with the movement of the penis or the man's pelvic bone in certain intercourse positions.

Sometimes, women who have not already experienced orgasm consider altering or removing their clitoral hood with the idea that this will make them orgasmic. This type of operation is rarely useful and may create problems rather than solve them.

Now, spread your inner lips and look at the area around your vagina. Locate your *urethra,* the small opening through which urine passes. This is above your vaginal opening. Take a good look at your *vagina.* Notice the shape of the opening, its color and texture. As you're looking at your vagina try clenching or contracting the muscle around your vagina. This is called the *pubococcygeous muscle.* If you are contracting the right muscle, you will probably be able to see some movement just inside the vaginal opening. Don't worry if you don't see anything. We will be talking more about these important muscles in the next chapter.

The area between the bottom of the vaginal opening and the *anus* or *rectum* is called the *perineum.* Often, this is where stitches are placed after childbirth. The *anus* is also surrounded by powerful muscles. Like other openings into the body such as the ears, mouth, nose, and vagina, the anus is often sensitive to erotic pleasure.

When you've completed your exploration, take a few minutes to relax. Close your eyes and breathe deeply a few turns. Inhale slowly and exhale. Rest for a minute and tune into any feelings you have from what you have just experienced.

1. How did you feel as you were looking at your genitals?

2. What did you like or dislike about what you saw?

3. Were you surprised by anything you discovered about your genital area?

It would be natural for you to have felt somewhat uncomfortable or embarrassed as you did this. Many women have never looked closely at their genitals or have only looked at times when they had to: after the delivery of a baby or when experiencing genital discomfort or pain. This seems amazing if you think about how often you have looked at other areas of your body. Perhaps the idea of really looking has never occurred to you, or you may have gotten the message as you were growing up that nice girls don't do that. So don't be concerned if you feel somewhat uncomfortable doing this or if you weren't impressed by your genitals at first sight. You will begin to feel more comfortable with this important part of your body as you become more familiar with it. This is just the beginning of what we hope will be a long friendship.

Try repeating this exercise again in a few days. Also, take advantage of those times when you have a natural opportunity to look at yourself—for example, while bathing or dressing or undresssing.

What did you like or dislike about what you saw? Did anything surprise you?

First, let's talk about some of the things you may have discovered about yourself. Some women are surprised to learn that the urethra, which passes urine from our bodies, is separate from the vagina. Even though it is, you probably noticed that the two openings are close to each other. Because of this, the urethra is stimulated during sexual arousal due to increased blood flow and vaginal tension and during intercourse by the movement of the penis in the vagina. For this reason, women often experience a desire to urinate during or just after sexual stimulation. Being sure to urinate after intercourse is a good idea because infections of the vagina will often spread to the urethra and bladder or vice versa. Burning, itching sensations, or painful urination should always be checked out with your doctor.

Women are often suprised by the shape and size of their vaginal opening. This is probably due to the fact that the vagina is often described in books and drawings (as well as in jokes or slang terms) as a kind of open hole. As you can see, it is actually more of a closed space, although the opening may be a little larger in women who've given birth to several children.

In its unaroused state, the walls of the vagina almost touch each other. The vaginal muscles are very flexible, however, and easily open to accommodate a man's penis. Arousal causes an increased flow of blood to the genitals and the diameter and length of the vagina increases. For these reasons, it's not necessary for you to be concerned about the actual size of your vagina or the size of a man's penis, since various sizes tend to accommodate each other. other. (More on this in Chapter 10.) However, keeping your vaginal muscles healthy and strong is important, and we've included some exercises for this in the next chapter.

Perhaps you noticed some moisture or secretion as you explored your genitals. This is natural, since there is always some lubrication in the vagina, although the normal amount varies from woman to woman. This lubrication is secreted by the walls of the vagina and helps protect it from irritation and infection. It's a good idea for you to learn what normal healthy secretion or lubrication looks like for you. Certain oral contraceptives will increase or decrease the amount of lubrication you have, as will age or certain illnesses. Also, vaginal infections can often be detected by noticeable changes in the amount, consistency, or smell of your secretions. Any such change, or itching or irritation of the genitals should be immediately checked out with your doctor.

When the vagina is healthy (when there are no infections) most lubrication has a faint smell which is not unpleasant. Regular washing of your genitals with soap and water is all that you really need to do in order to keep your genitals clean. Commercial deodorant sprays for your external genitals are not necessary and have been found to irritate the delicate skin of many women. Your natural vaginal odor is probably mild and not noticeable to others except perhaps during sex. At those times, the natural smell of clean healthy genitals can be a source of pleasurable erotic stimulation for your partner.

Douching or cleansing of the vagina with water or other solutions or the insertion of vaginal suppositories for this purpose is also a practice that doctors have found increasingly unnecessary. Douching was practiced at one time as a form of contraception, but (largely because it is not effective) it is rarely recommended for this purpose today. Most often douching is recommended by physicians in order to treat vaginal infections with solutions that need to be applied inside the vagina. Douching regularly with commercial products as a way to cleanse yourself or deal with concerns about genital odor is likely to do more harm than good. Strong douche solutions tend to interfere with your body's natural lubricating protection against infection.

Often, women are surprised that their genitals did not seem ugly or unpleasant looking to them. They report being curious about the different colors and the delicate look of their skin. Sometimes, however, women do find this experience (particularly if they've never looked closely at themselves before) upsetting.

Perhaps you found you were unable even to complete the exercise. That's okay. You need to spend a little more time getting comfortable. Start by looking at the drawings of women's genitals we've included in this book. Try seeing if you can notice the differences between them. Next see if one picture makes you less uncomfortable than the others. What about this picture makes you less uncomfortable? Then, see if one of the pictures reminds you of your own genitals. What about it is similar to your genitals? After becoming more comfortable with the pictures, try another session where you look at your genitals. You may be surprised to find it a little easier. If not, we suggest you skip ahead to Chapter 3 and practice the exercises for relaxation. After you feel you are able to effectively relax yourself, try another session where you look at your genitals.

If you were able to look at your genitals but found it upsetting, try to give yourself credit for having done this exercise at all. And even though you may not feel the way you'd like to yet, at least you've made a start. Here are some suggestions which will help you to feel more positive about your genitals over a period of time.

1. As we suggested earlier, do this exercise again and take advantage of other opportunities to look at your genitals.

2. Try describing your genitals in words. What seemed unpleasant for you? One woman being seen in sex therapy described her genitals as "ugly and wrinkled . . . like the mouth of an old person." With this kind of image in her mind, it was not surprising that it was hard for her to feel anything but negative about her genitals. Try writing down your description. Look at the words you've chosen and the image that this creates in your mind. Now try creating another image that is somewhat more positive. For example, try looking at your genitals and comparing their shape to parts of a flower, or a shell, or a design.

   Thinking about this part of you in this way may seem strange to you now, but we have seen many women learn to appreciate their genitals as beautiful parts of themselves.

3. Try reading and doing some of the exercises for relaxation (Chapter 3) before your next "looking" session. Being relaxed may make it easier for you to begin to feel more comfortable.

4. If you still experience a great deal of difficulty, you may want to move ahead to the next chapter. We will continue throughout this book to deal with your feelings about yourself, your body, and the experiences you have had. So don't feel you must change drastically right now. Remember, change can be a slow process, and it's important to feel good about yourself for the things you *can do now.*

3

Exploration by Touch

In the last chapter you began to learn more about yourself by examining your past and the ways in which it has influenced your attitudes towards sex. Also, you began looking more closely at your body and exploring yourself visually.

In this chapter you're going to continue this exploration in two ways—by expanding your experience both through your sense of touch and through exercises designed to increase your awareness of sensations in your body.

Touch plays an important role in our ability to enjoy sensual feelings. Touch allows us to experience what we cannot see or hear—the textures and temperatures of our environment. What differences are there between touching a real orchid, a plastic orchid, and a colored photograph of an orchid? Suppose you hear a kitten purring; what difference does it make when you actually hold it while it purrs? Our sense of touch and our ability to perceive sensations can provide both information and pleasure about ourselves. As you do the exercises in this chapter, try thinking of your body as a new world to be explored, full of different textures and shapes.

To do this exercise, choose a time when you feel good (not worried or hassled) and can spend 30 minutes to an hour by yourself. Have on hand some body lotion, oil, or powder that you like. You may want to start with a relaxing bath or shower. When you're done, stay nude and find a comfortable spot where you can lie or sit reclining your back against something for support—your bed, some cushions on the floor, or your couch, if you have the living room to yourself. (You may want to spread a towel out under you if you are using an oil or lotion.) Now apply some body lotion, powder, or oil onto your arms and legs. Slowly begin exploring your body all over—your arms, hands, feet, legs, breasts, stomach, the inside of your thighs. You may want to close your eyes as you do this or you may like the idea of looking at yourself in a mirror. See if you can really focus in on what you're feeling. How do your hands feel going over each part of your body? Tune out other things. Let your hands experiment with different ways to touch—use your fingertips for a while, and then try the palms of your hands or your wrists.

What do different areas of your body feel like to you? Is one area soft and smooth, another muscular, another rough? Notice sharp, angular places, curves, and fullness. If you like, turn on your stomach and feel your buttocks and the back of your legs. Change position as often as you like. Spend around 10 minutes or so on these parts of your body and then let your hands slide along the inside of your thighs to your genitals.

Take your time. Let your fingers explore your pubic hair; notice its texture. Is it soft or coarse? Then touch the soft skin of your outer lips and the muscular area between your vagina and anus (the perineum). Move your finger tips into the moist inner lips. Compare the feel of the outside surface to the inner area of the lips. What does the skin here feel like to you? Does it feel like any other parts of your body? Don't try for any particular feelings, just be aware of the shapes and textures.

Then explore your clitoral shaft and see if you can feel your clitoris through the clitoral hood. Pull the hood back and lightly touch your clitoris. Trace the outer edge of your vagina. Let your fingers go inside your vagina to the moist warmth. Do you feel any muscles inside your vagina? Try contracting the ring of vaginal muscles you looked at in the last exercise. Can you feel it contracting around your finger? Explore the walls of your vagina. Is the texture smooth or rough, flat or ridged?

You may want to go back to touching some of the rest of your body again as a way of ending this exercise. Take a few deep breaths. Inhale slowly for three counts. Exhale slowly for three counts. When you are ready, think about the following questions:

1. How did you feel touching your genitals? (Did you feel comfortable, awkward, silly, shy, embarrassed, disgusted?)

2. How did you feel touching the other parts of your body? Describe these feelings.

3. Did you learn anything new about yourself?

Perhaps you felt comfortable doing this exercise or touching certain parts of your body, or you may have been uncomfortable through all or part of this exercise. These feelings are natural. Usually we touch ourselves for functional reasons: dressing, washing, scratching, or tending to a cut or bruise. It may be difficult for you to feel that it's all right to touch your body, especially your genitals, for the purpose of learning about yourself. Repeating this exercise a second time can help allay these uncomfortable feelings. You may feel less awkward and embarrassed and your body will seem more familiar to you.

Something else which will help you feel more comfortable now, as well as throughout this growth program, is learning some ways to relax yourself.

EXERCISES FOR RELAXATION

You may feel that you know how to relax quite well. Most people, however, do have times when tension takes over, when their bodies and their minds are "uptight." At these times it is particularly difficult to really let yourself experience pleasant feelings. The following pages includes some exercises that will help you learn to recognize tension in your body and some ways to relax yourself. They are also useful for another reason—in using them, you can develop a better ability to focus on and appreciate sensations of all types throughout your body.

If you felt comfortable during the exercises in Chapters 2 and 3 (Looking at Yourself, and Exploration by Touch), do the "Deep Muscle" relaxation exercise *three to five times a week* for two weeks or until you feel you can relax yourself fairly easily. The "Muscle Control" exercise is optional for you.

If you felt uncomfortable during the exercises in Chapters 2 and 3, do the following "Deep Muscle" relaxation exercise *once or twice a day* for two weeks. As soon as you feel ready, you may want to go back and repeat the exercises in Chapters 2 and 3 that made you uncomfortable or that you were unable to do. This time you should feel more relaxed and enjoy your session. If you have difficulty doing the Deep Muscle relaxation exercise, go on to Exercise 2, Muscle Control. Practice this exercise, and when you feel ready, go back and try the Deep Muscle relaxation exercise. When you can do this comfortably, you may want to repeat those exercises that were difficult for you again. You should feel more relaxed and at ease this time.

EXERCISE 1: DEEP MUSCLE RELAXATION

This is an effective technique which will give you a way to relax yourself whenever you feel the need. You shouldn't expect yourself to be able to do it perfectly the first few times. Think of this exercise as a skill that needs to be practiced.

Before beginning, make sure you have 15-30 minutes to spend without interruptions. The first few times you do this you will need to open your eyes occasionally in order to read these directions. After you become familiar with the steps, you won't need to refer to the directions and you can keep your eyes closed throughout the exercise.

You may want to begin by taking a warm bath, turning on some soft background music, or doing whatever you've learned helps you relax. If you are dressed, make sure your clothes are loosened. Take off your shoes and your glasses or contact lenses, if you wear them.

Choose a place to relax in that is relatively quiet and will help you to concentrate only on yourself. Create an environment for yourself where you feel comfortable; some things you might think about are lighting, room temperature, and music.

You'll want to find a place to sit or lie which will leave your body as supported and tension-free as possible (a bed, couch, reclining chair, or cushions arranged with some support for your back and head).

Now let your arms and hands hang or rest in a loose relaxed manner. Let your head lean back against its support. Close your eyes. Try to relax deeply. Make your body heavy. Begin by tensing your forehead. See if you can wrinkle it into a deep frown. Feel the tension in your forehead, the pull on your scalp, the feeling of pressure. Now relax these muscles. Feel your forehead become smooth, your scalp relax. Concentrate on the feeling of relaxation.

Now, tense the muscles around your eyes and nose by closing your eyes as tightly as possible. You don't have to tense your muscles so much that they cramp. Just tighten up enough to feel the tension so that you can notice the difference when you relax. Feel the tension in your eyebrows and the bridge of your nose. Focus on the tension. Now relax. Feel the tension flowing from around your eyes and your nose, each part becoming quiet and smooth. Enjoy this feeling of relaxation. Try tensing your lips and jaws by clenching your teeth together. Feel the pressure on your gums. Hold the tension. Focus on the tension. Now relax. Flow with the relaxation. Notice the different sensations accompanying relaxation. Enjoy the feeling of relaxation that is becoming more and more evident in your head and face.

Now press the back of your head against its support. Study the tension in your neck. Notice the sensations of tension and strain. Now relax. Let your head hang limp and loose for a moment. Let it feel heavy and loose and relaxed, then tense again and note the difference between when you're tense and when you are relaxed. Now relax. Feel the muscles in your neck become smooth and quiet. Now tense the front of your neck by pushing your chin into your chest. Feel the tension in your neck and throat. Focus on the tension. Notice the sensations. Now relax and breathe deeply. Let yourself enjoy the feeling of becoming more and more relaxed. Your forehead and eyes, nose and jaws, cheeks and neck should feel smooth and quiet. Now in the same way, relax and tense the following muscle groups:

a. Hands, by clenching them.
b. Wrists and forearms, by extending them and bending the hands back at the wrists.
c. Shoulders, by shrugging them.
d. Chest, by taking a deep breath and holding it, then exhaling.
e. Back, by arching the back up and away from the support surface.
f. Stomach, by sucking it in and forming it into a tight knot.
g. Hips and buttocks, by pressing buttocks together tightly.
h. Thighs, by clenching them.
i. Lower legs, by pointing the toes and curling toes downward.

When you are done, stay in touch with your feelings for a few minutes. When you are ready to get up, take a few deep breaths, open your eyes and get up slowly. Stretch your whole body.

—Were you able to distinguish any particular areas of tension that you were not aware of before? Describe them.
—Did you experience difficulty relaxing any specific muscle group? If so, concentrate on these areas during your next practice session.

If you had problems—perhaps you were tensing your *whole* body rather than one specific group of muscles at a time. If you think this may be so, go to the next exercise and practice it. When you can do the Muscle Control Exercise successfully, come back to this exercise and try it again.

If you felt sleepy and found it hard to continue, make sure you are not doing this exercise when you are tired or just before going to bed. If you used your bed or bedroom, try repeating this exercise in another part of the house.

If your trouble was that *you couldn't concentrate* and your mind wandered or your thoughts interfered, you need practice on focusing your attention. Try and clear your mind of distracting thoughts. If this is too difficult, you may want to postpone your sessions for another time. Another exercise, Body Awareness, will also help you learn to shut out distracting thoughts. We explain this in a moment.

EXERCISE 2: MUSCLE CONTROL

This set of exercises increases your control of specific muscles. When you learn any physical skill, you train certain muscle groups to perform. Often, how well you do depends on keeping other muscles relaxed. This allows you to make the most of your energy.

1. In order to gain control of the different muscles of your body, you need to be able to identify them and tell them apart. Lie on your back with a pillow(s) under your head and knees. Now, begin tensing your body, *one part* at a time. Begin with your feet. Contract your feet, then your calves, thighs, buttocks, fingers, hands, arms, shoulders, neck, and face. Concentrate on the sensation of tension in each body part. Now, relax each muscle group, *one part* at a time. Relax your feet, calves, thighs, buttocks, fingers, hands, arms, shoulders, neck, and face. Do this sequence three times.

2. The next step is to learn to contract one muscle while relaxing all other muscles. Lie down as before. Contract and tense your right arm but keep the rest of your body relaxed. Hold this for the count of 10. Relax your arm. Do the following sequence, concentrating on tensing *only* those muscles listed and keeping the rest of your body loose and relaxed:

    a. Contract right arm.
    b. Contract left arm.
    c. Contract right leg.
    d. Contract left leg.
    e. Contract right arm *and* right leg.
    f. Contract left arm *and* left leg.
    g. Contract both arms.
    h. Contract both legs.

Remember, keep the rest of your body relaxed! Now go on and try these:

a. Contract right arm and left leg.
b. Contract right leg and left arm.

This exercise is even easier to master with someone helping you. After trying it out the first time by yourself, you may want to do this with your partner or a friend. Their job is to tell you which muscle groups to tense and to check to make sure the rest of your body is relaxed. This can be done by slightly lifting the untensed leg or arm and seeing how loose and relaxed it feels. However, you can master this on your own if you choose to.

Practice this for a few days. If you had trouble with Deep Muscle Relaxation, go back and try it again. You will probably have better control over your muscles now and should be able to tense particular muscle groups while keeping the rest of your body relaxed. If you did both exercises, you probably noticed some differences. Which did you like better? How did each make you feel? Do you feel either of these works well for you?

Some people find that muscle relaxation exercises seem to make them more tense rather than more relaxed. If this was true for you, try the *Body Awareness Exercise* below. Again, try reading through the procedure first and then close your eyes and visualize the various scenes. You may want to write a one or two word description of each and keep it near you if you need to refer to it. Or you might record the procedure on tape and play it back while you go through the scenes. Another possibility is to ask another person to read them to you as you are relaxing. We suggest that you make a tape or have someone read them to you if possible. Remember to pause about 10 seconds between each question.

Begin by making yourself comfortable. As you or someone else asks each question of you, let yourself become totally immersed in each scene. Try and let your total concentration be involved for several seconds (5–10 seconds perhaps) in the particular image.

EXERCISE 3: BODY AWARENESS

Is it possible for you to allow your eyes to close? If they are not yet closed, you may close them now. Can you be aware of the point at which the back of your head comes in contact with the chair?

Is it possible for you to imagine the space between your eyes?

Is it possible for you to be aware how close your breath comes to the back of your eyes every time you inhale?

Can you imagine that you are looking at something that is very far away?

Is it possible for you to be aware of the points where your arms are in contact with the chair and can you be aware of the points at which your arms lose contact with the chair?

Is either your left or right foot resting on the floor; and if either or both of them are, can you feel the floor beneath your foot?

Can you imagine in your mind's eye a beautiful flower suspended a few feet in front of you? Is it possible for you to close your lids of your inner eye so that you can no longer see the flower?

Is it possible for you to be aware of the space within your mouth? And can you be aware of the position of your tongue within your mouth?

Is it possible for you to feel even the slightest breeze against your cheek?

Are you aware of one of your arms being heavier than the other?

Is there a tingling or feeling of numbness in one of your hands?

Are you aware of one of your arms being more relaxed than the other?

Is it possible for you to notice any change in the temperature of your body?

Is your left arm warmer than your right?

Is it possible for you to feel like a rag doll?

Can you be aware of your left forearm? Can you feel any tightness in it?

Is it possible for you to imagine something that is *very pleasant* for you?

Can you feel yourself floating as if on a cloud? Or are you feeling much too heavy for that?

Can your arms feel very heavy, as if they were stuck in molasses?

Is it possible for you to imagine once again that you are looking at something that is very far away?

Is there a heaviness coming into your legs?

Is it possible for you to imagine yourself floating in warm water?

Can you feel the weight of your body in the chair?

Can you allow yourself just to drift along lazily?

Is it possible for you to imagine in your mind's eye another beautiful flower? Can you notice what color the flower is if you see one? Can you close the lids of your inner eye so that you no longer see the flower?

Is it possible to notice whether one of your arms is heavier than the other, and can you notice whether one of your legs is heavier than the other?

Can you allow your eyes to open; and if they're not yet open you may open them now and be wide awake and very comfortable.

How did you feel about doing this? Were you able to visualize the scenes? Did you feel you became more relaxed?

Whichever relaxation procedure works best for you, practice it regularly until you feel you can quickly and easily relax yourself after a while. You will find that you do not need to go through the entire procedure, but that just a few minutes relaxing particular areas of your body or visualizing certain scenes will be enough.

VAGINAL EXERCISES (KEGELS)

In the last exercise, you tried to contract your vaginal muscles. The names of these amazing muscles again are the pubococcygeal muscles. These muscles are important to your health, and they also play a part in increasing vaginal sensations.

Your genital muscles need exercise just as your other muscles do. In 1952, some exercises were developed by Arnold Kegel for women who were having urinary continence and other related problems. It was found that in these women the pubococcygeus muscle was "out of shape" and could not function properly. Exercising this muscle eliminated the medical problems, and, to everyone's surprise, also seemed to increase the potential for genital sensation and orgasm. Part of the reason for this is probably the fact that blood flow increases to muscles which are exercised, and that increased blood flow is related to the ease of arousal and orgasm. Learning these exercises will help you keep these muscles functioning while also increasing your feelings of genital pleasure.

Remember, these exercises will require some concentration at first; but they will become routine after a short time. When you first try these exercises, start by contracting this muscle while urinating. See if you can stop and start your urine mid-flow. Make sure your legs are fairly well apart so you'll be sure you're using the correct set of muscles. After you've done this a couple of times, finish emptying your bladder. You *should not* continue to exercise when you urinate because this procedure sometimes does not allow the bladder to empty as fully as it should, and this may lead to infection.

Now that you've located the muscles, try doing your exercises while standing, sitting, or lying down. They can be done anywhere at any time. No one but you will know. A good idea is to set aside a certain time each day when you will practice these, and work in additional practice when and where you can. Occasionally, check to make sure you are not using your abdominal muscles too, by resting your hand on your abdomen as you do the contractions. When you have learned to do them easily, you can do them almost anytime—while you're driving, brushing your teeth, or whatever.

Since these muscles may be weak, you may not feel the muscle contracting or tightening at first. If you're not sure anything is happening, insert one or your fingers into your vagina. You will probably be able to feel your muscles contracting if you're exercising correctly. Don't be concerned if you can't, however. After you've practiced these exercises for a while you will probably be able to feel the contractions.

VAGINAL EXERCISES (KEGELS)

1. Contract the muscle, hold for a count of three, then relax. Breathe regularly.

2. Contract the muscle while inhaling, pulling the muscle upward with the intake of breath. This may be harder to do, because you may find your stomach muscles contracting as well. With time you will learn to do this one without contracting the stomach muscles.

3. Contract and relax the muscle as quickly as possible, while breathing regularly.

4. Bear down on the muscle as if pushing something out of the vagina, or trying to urinate in a hurry. You may find yourself holding your breath, but try to breathe regularly.

You may notice a warm or full feeling in your genitals as you do these exercises. This is probably due to the flow of blood to this area. You may or may not experience pleasurable feelings as you do these. Each woman is different in how her body responds to these exercises. The important thing is not to try to make yourself feel a particular way. Just relax, and focus in on what you *are* feeling. Remember, the purpose of these exercises is to help you build a healthier body and to tune you into feelings and sensations in your genitals—whether they be pleasant, unpleasant, or neutral. This awareness is the first step in gaining understanding of, and some control over, your body and its responses.

HOW OFTEN SHOULD YOU DO THEM?

Find a convenient time every day to practice. These exercises become easier to do with time, and they only take a few minutes a day. During the first week, do each exercise ten times, *twice a day.*

Continue to do these exercises *at least once per day, for the remainder of the growth program.* Actually, continuing on a regular basis throughout your life is one way of maintaining healthy vaginal and urinary muscles.

When you feel comfortable with what you've done in this chapter (anywhere from a few days to a week or so) go on to Chapter 4.

4

Touching for Pleasure: Discovery

What do you think of when you hear the word pleasure? Perhaps you think of something physical—a massage, a dip in a swimming pool on a hot day—or something that involves your feelings and emotions—the anticipation of an upcoming vacation, the company of a good friend, or the satisfaction of doing something well.

Often, pleasure may be the combination of physical sensations and emotions: savoring a delicious meal, playing tennis, or taking a walk on a beautiful day. Sensual and sexual pleasure is also the result of an interaction between physical sensations and your thoughts, feelings, and attitudes.

The particular combination of things that evokes feelings of pleasure in you is uniquely your own. You learn what these are through a wide range of experiences and exploration over the course of your life. As we explained earlier though, it is not unusual for women to grow up with little knowledge of their body's capacity for sensual, sexual pleasure. Without this knowledge, you've probably found yourself frustrated and at a loss to express your sexual preferences during lovemaking. Knowing how to give pleasure to your body, and accepting pleasure from it, can help you to get what you want for yourself sexually.

How do you feel when you think about exploring your body for areas and ways of touching that will feel pleasurable? For many women, this is a new idea, or an idea which they've been taught to ignore or repress. You may think of your body as something which should give pleasure to someone else, and the idea that *you* can enjoy your body for yourself may seem somehow immoral or wrong. Thinking back to your goals for yourself and this program may be helpful for you at this point. Sexual growth and the development of more enjoyable sexual expression with or without a partner has to start with self knowledge.

Let's take a few minutes and look at what you've accomplished up to this point. By now you've spent some time thinking about your attitudes and feelings that are related to sex. You've looked at your body and explored its contours and textures. You've probably come a long way in terms of how comfortable you feel and how aware you are of your body. Becoming familiar with special places on your body and knowing how to touch them in order to provide sensual or sexual pleasure is the next step. Learning these unique things about yourself will help make it possible for you to achieve sexual fulfillment and satisfaction on your own or with a partner. Why? There are several reasons.

Knowing where and how to touch your body for pleasure means that you will be able to share this information with your partner. (This is discussed in Chapters 8 and 9.) This will enhance the quality of sexual experiences for you both.

Also, research has shown that for many women, the easiest and strongest orgasms occur during self-pleasuring (masturbation). For women who have not yet experienced orgasm, masturbation often provides the kind of stimulation most likely to lead to feelings of arousal and orgasm.

Since masturbation is a good way to experience frequent orgasms, the orgasmic response has a chance to become well established. Blood flow to the genitals increases as your body learns this new skill. This means that orgasm is more and more likely to occur. Also, the more orgasms you have, the more comfortable you will feel about trusting yourself and letting your feelings flow.

Yet knowing all of the "facts" and all of the advantages to be gained does not necessarily make it easy for many women to overcome feelings that have been ingrained since childhood about masturbation. Often these feelings and attitudes are the result of misinformation and myths about the supposed harms of masturbation. Rather than being "abnormal," masturbation is just another normal and natural expression of sexuality. Most men and women masturbate at some time during their lives. Contrary to old myths, masturbation does not cause psychological or physical harm. Rather, it provides a healthy release for sexual tension and is a good opportunity to learn about (or keep in touch with) your sexuality. Perhaps you've been taught that masturbation is immature—something that you did as a child, but shouldn't do as an adult or after you are married. Actually, masturbation is something that many mature people engage in from time to time, married or not.

One concern people often have is that masturbating will reduce their desire for sex with their partner. There is no physiological basis for this belief, since achieving orgasm through masturbation is no more "draining" than an orgasm achieved through intercourse or some other activity with a partner. Studies have shown that masturbation can have a *positive* influence on sexual relationships with a partner. It has been found that women who are orgasmic through any means before marriage, including masturbation, often have less difficulty experiencing orgasm with their partner after marriage. Women who have no orgasmic experience have more difficulty becoming orgasmic with a partner.

Finally, women sometimes express the fear that they will

become dependent on masturbation; that they will desire to masturbate too much or only experience orgasm in this way. In our experience seeing women in therapy, there is no such thing as "too much" sex. Women are usually able to use what they learn through masturbation to enrich the quality of their sexual relationship with their partner. Ways to do this are discussed in Chapter 8–10. Because they are more aware of their bodies' and their own sexual responsiveness, these women usually become orgasmic through other forms of stimulation such as manual caressing by their partner and oral-genital sex.

Temporarily, try putting your concerns aside for a moment so that you can continue the exploration and growth process you began in Chapter 2. Often, with time and practice, an activity that is initially difficult and uncomfortable becomes easier and more a part of you. Self-pleasuring or masturbation may be something you only do in the context of this exploration and sexual growth program. Or you may choose to continue masturbation after you have completed this program. This is for you to decide. These exercises are only vehicles which can help you get to where *you* want to grow.

DISCOVERING PLEASURE

Begin by reserving 30 minutes to an hour for yourself. Relax in a way which you enjoy and which you've found works well for you—perhaps a bath or relaxation exercises. The room you will be in should help create a relaxing atmosphere for you (pleasing lighting, incense, or other small details which make a difference to you). *Be good to yourself;* you should feel free to be as fussy about the trimmings for your own session as you would be if a real lover were joining you.

Use some body lotion, oil, or powder, as you explore yourself. Warming the lotion or oil is easy to do by setting the bottle in hot water; this gives the liquid a nice feeling as you smooth it on your body. You might start with your arms and hands and move down to the rest of your body, or start with your feet and legs if you prefer. Focus your attention on the feel of your hand on your body. Massage and touch yourself in different ways. Try to help your body feel good—don't try for arousal. Let your hand touch your breasts, abdomen, inner

thighs. Try some of the different strokes and ways of touching you began to explore in the last chapter. Be gentle with yourself, and try to tune into any feelings of pleasure your body is giving you.

Let your hand find your labia and clitoral shaft. Stroke your lips lightly, run your finger alongside the clitoris and up over the shaft. Massage the clitoris lightly between two fingers or try a circular motion on the clitoris. You may want to explore with one or both of your hands at the same time. Or use one hand on one part of your body and your other hand on another. Vary your strokes and rhythm and move to new areas. Explore different parts of your body for pleasurable feelings—try your arms and the inside of your legs as well as your breasts and clitoris. Touch just inside your vagina to see how this feels. Focus on feelings—stay with areas that feel good or better than others. Share your body with yourself. When you feel ready to end this session, try lightly massaging any areas of tension until you feel relaxed and good all over. Close your eyes and take some deep full breaths, inhaling through your nose, exhaling through your mouth.

How did you feel about this experience? Were you more, or less, comfortable than you expected?

Women react in different ways to the exercise above. You may have felt curious, afraid, guilty, repulsed, excited, or nervous. Perhaps you were aware of several feelings. Sometimes these are the result of watching yourself almost as if you were a spectator observing what you were doing from a distance. You may have thought about how awkward or silly you looked doing this, or how other people would respond if they knew what you were doing.

This tendency to take the role of the spectator is a natural result of feelings of anxiety or embarrassment and often occurs at the beginning of any process for change. Refocusing your attention back on your body and what it is feeling will help you deal with the tendency to be a spectator. In the next chapter you will learn more specific ways to improve your ability to become totally involved in your self-pleasuring.

Were you expecting (or putting pressure on yourself) to feel arousal?

It's very easy to become caught up in going after arousal. However, this usually results in your becoming an observer of your responses rather than a participant in your pleasure. You may find yourself worrying about how well you're doing and putting pressure on yourself to try harder. This interferes with whatever pleasure you might experience.

For now, try to relax and let yourself experience whatever it is your body is feeling. If you aren't aware of any pleasurable feelings right now, that's all right. It may take you a while to learn to label the different feelings you may be experiencing. For now, try focusing on any areas that feel different from others and noticing your reaction to different ways of touching yourself.

If you were extremely upset or repulsed by this activity, you need to go more slowly. Keep in mind the reasons why it's important for you to have this knowledge about yourself, and your original reasons for wanting to embark on this program for sexual growth.

Try coming back to this exercise when you feel you want to attempt it again. Relax yourself first by doing one or more of the relaxation exercises from Chapter 3. At first spend only a few minutes of self-pleasuring and gradually increase the time as you begin to feel more comfortable.

SOME ADDITIONAL SUGGESTIONS

To make each session a real exploration in pleasure, try varying some of the following:

Where you have your session. If you have privacy in rooms other than your bedroom, you might try these areas. One woman who followed this program enjoyed doing her touching for the first few sessions while in a warm bath.

Your position. You may want to sit up or lie on your stomach or side. You may also enjoy the feel of a pillow under different parts of your body.

Use some kind of gentle lubricant. Baby oil, secretions from your vagina, saliva—all may be enjoyable and add to your sensitivity. However, be cautious of anything with perfume or other strong ingredients. The skin of your genitals is extremely sensitive, and alcohol or other additives in lotions or oils may irritate or cause a burning sensation. A good thing to try is a water soluble jel called "K–Y" or "Lubrifax." These are available in drugstores and you do not need a prescription to buy them. These are the *only* things (except saliva or your natural secretions) which should be used while you're exploring the *inside* of your vagina. It will not irritate you or interfere with your body's natural lubrication. It is *not* a good idea to use vaseline petroleum jelly, since it is not water soluble and tends to interfere with natural vaginal protection against infection.

Vary the amount of time you spend. Be flexible within the 15–30 minutes, concentrating on different areas and spending the amount of time that feels comfortable for you.

Try exploring other textures and feelings. For example, the feel of a rough towel, or of a piece of velvet or a silk scarf rubbed alone your body. Be as inventive and creative as you like. Explore ways to awaken your body—keeping "discovery" an active part of your sessions prevents them from becoming mechanical or a chore.

Vary the time of day during which you have your session. Try mornings, afternoons, late and early evenings if you can. You may find that your body is more responsive at certain times. This also allows you to be more spontaneous, to take advantage of good times to have a session whenever they occur, and to have sessions when you feel like it. (This may not be possible very often if you have many responsibilities.)

Try to repeat this exploration two times over the next week. Spend 15 to 30 minutes each time. When you feel that you have learned about the pleasurable areas of your body and ways to touch them, go on to Chapter 5. If you feel uncomfortable doing this exercise or if you are not able to distinguish any pleasurable feelings, give yourself more time. Spend another week or so on this and then move on to Chapter 5.

Some women enjoy the feelings that come from pressing their legs together tightly. Occasionally, a woman will be orgasmic using this type of stimulation. The problem with this seems to be that it is often difficult for these women to become orgasmic through partner stimulation. This makes sense, since there is no way a partner can pleasure you in this way; and intercourse particularly may interfere with the pattern of thigh pressure. For this reason, we don't encourage exploration of this type of stimulation right now. At some later time, when you are orgasmic through other ways, you may want to include this. However, you should be able to experience feelings of pleasure in your genitals in ways other than through thigh pressure.

If you have been using thigh pressure stimulation and find it difficult to get pleasure from other forms of touching, there are several things you can try. Since thigh pressure provides a lot of indirect stimulation from tensing certain muscles, you might concentrate on providing pressure to your mons area with several fingers or the entire palm of your hand, rather than stimulate the clitoris and vaginal area directly. At the same time, *without* clenching your legs together, you can tense your buttocks and leg muscles. Practicing this should provide you with pleasurable feelings and also allow you to increase the variety of ways to be stimulated. It will probably take a while to learn to enjoy this, so be patient if the first few attempts are not as satisfying as your old method.

5

Touching for Pleasure: Focusing

The last chapter was a beginning in self-discovery. Perhaps you feel like you have made a good start in learning what areas of your body are especially likely to give you pleasure, and what kinds of touching are best suited to different parts of your body. Or perhaps you feel that you haven't found out anything new and that your body is not really providing any pleasurable sensations even though you continue to try in different ways. We all have different patterns of growth; sometimes changing is a gradual process, sometimes it goes in spurts. You have your own unique pattern, so try to appreciate how you make gains rather than becoming impatient with how fast those changes take place.

Meanwhile, there are a variety of things that this chapter can offer you that we feel will give you a chance to expand your ability to give yourself pleasure. We will be discussing ways in which you might improve your concentration during your self-pleasuring sessions, and we will give you some aids for getting into the mood to have a session. For instance, we will talk about some body exercises you can do to feel physically looser and more agile, and also to become more comfortable with sexual tension and movement during sex. We will also share with you some exercises that other women have found to be helpful for increasing their mental ability to focus on sensual-sexual sensations.

You will continue to experiment with your self-pleasuring sessions; and we hope that you begin to feel more comfortable about letting yourself touch your genitals for pleasure, and that you develop a clearer understanding of how different kinds of stimulation affect you at different times. Of course, you will not learn all of this the first time you try. Your body may respond a little differently each time, but it always provides you with information about what does or doesn't feel good. Give yourself at least three or four sessions in order to become comfortable and learn several ways of stimulating yourself.

When you do find that you are having difficulty getting in the mood for experiencing pleasure in some of your self-pleasuring sessions, it's important to remind yourself that this does not mean that you are a failure. Rather, you are learning important information—from those times when you can't seem to get anywhere, try and learn something about *why* it's difficult. Has something upsettting happened earlier in the day? Do you feel pressed for time? Do your thoughts wander? As you attempt to identify at what point your progress seems to slow down, we will be offering suggestions regarding several of the more frequent trouble spots.

Some women have commented that they are really not sure if they are experiencing pleasure or not, particularly when they are touching their genitals. "It's different," one woman said, "but I'm not sure if it's pleasurable or neutral." If these are new feelings for you, you may find it difficult to label them at first. Whatever sensations you detect, explore them (as long as they are not unpleasant) and let them continue, no matter how small the difference or the pleasure may be for you. Give yourself plenty of time and a number of different occasions to develop the kinds of stimulation that you like. If you do feel pleasure or sexual arousal for a few seconds and then lose the sensations, don't worry: This is a natural pattern, especially when you are beginning to experience sexual feelings.

GETTING STARTED

Try having one 30 minute session now or later on today. Take your usual preparations that will assure that you have some time to yourself. Touch and stroke various areas of your body, and then begin to focus on the most pleasurable areas, including your genitals. Then just try to continue letting pleasurable feeling flow with whatever touches seem to work.

After you finish, think over the following questions:

What were the most difficult parts of this step? Try to identify what went well and what seems to cause you difficulty. Common areas of difficulty include: a) Getting into the mood for a session. Are you allowing yourself uninterrupted time during a time of the day when you are not fatigued or pressed to do other things? b) Do you find your mind wandering and is it difficult to concentrate on yourself? Do you find that c) it is difficult to feel very sensual about stimulating your genitals— perhaps it seems a little mechanical and no stroke feels better than any other? You may be expecting too much progress too fast. Try being more patient with yourself and seeing if you can come up with some ways of your own (again, we'll be helping you) to make the experience more sensual.

It is also possible that you are still having some negative feelings about the whole idea of masturbation, and this could make it difficult for you to let yourself experience pleasure in this way. Learning to deal with your reservations about masturbation (if it seems unnatural, or if you are afraid you will like it more than other kinds of sexual activity as you continue to do it) also takes time. Remember that the goal is to provide you with opportunities for you to learn about your body and the pleasure it can give you. Eventually you may only want to masturbate once in a while, or you may decide to masturbate more frequently; but that choice will be yours. Your sexuality is part of your expression as a person, and it will not suddenly take over and dominate every other aspect of your life. Nevertheless, whatever reservations you have about masturbating are real and important, and you don't have to get rid of them completely in order to continue your self-pleasuring explorations. Instead, we suggest that for now you think about a few of the positive things you can gain from learning to masturbate—for instance, feeling relaxed, feeling pleasure, becoming more sensual. Focus on the potential gains rather than focusing on the old feelings of why you shouldn't try.

What kinds of stimulation were most effective in giving you pleasure? When do you notice the most sensitivity or feeling— during what kinds of pressure, strokes, rhythms, and at what locations on your genitals does stimulation feel best? Good feelings often ebb and flow, so if you notice an area feeling numb or uncomfortable, try a different kind of touch or move to a different place.

Do you find yourself concerned about whether or not you will experience sexual arousal? This is perhaps one of the most tempting, and least helpful, occurrences during self-stimulation. When you find yourself mentally "watching" your own responses, try to stop those thoughts and refocus your thoughts on the feelings in your body. How is your body responding to what your hands are doing? Think of this as a kind of communication, with your hands and body responding to each other.

Not all of your sessions will be the same. Sometimes you will feel that nothing is happening; at other times you will feel you have made progress. This is a natural growth process that everyone experiences, so try not to put pressure on yourself if things seem to go slowly for you. It's important not to compare different sessions. Just try to treat each session as one more opportunity to learn about yourself. This isn't always easy, especially if you feel like you are not making any progress at all. If you do have a session that is difficult or unrewarding for you, try to do the following: a) Think about little details of your session and try to pick out a few "small" things that went a bit better than they have in the past—it may be simply feeling a little more comfortable touching yourself or enjoying a different kind of stimulation you hadn't noticed before. Give yourself credit for any aspects of your sessions that are showing even slight improvement. b) Think about what you can *learn* from a session that is disappointing for you. Think about what made it disappointing. Were your expectations too high? Did you try too hard? Did you have trouble concentrating or getting into the mood? Were you upset about something else when you began? Identifying some possible interferences is a beginning; doing something about it will come with time and patience.

WAYS TO FOCUS ON AND ENJOY SELF-PLEASURING

The following suggestions are included in order to help you to become more involved in your sessions—both mentally and physically—and to feel more in tune with your body in general. First, we will talk about some sensual *"loosening"* exercises. Then we will discuss *sensate focus* as a way to mentally tune into your physical sensations. And finally, we will talk a little about *erotic literature* and *fantasy*.

A FEW "LOOSENING" EXERCISES

The following exercises can benefit you in several ways. In doing them, you will be using muscles that are usually involved in sexual activities, so they should help you strengthen those muscles and get adjusted to the kind of physical tension that accompanies sexual arousal. Also, some of the exercises allow you to practice certain movements that occur during sexual activities. You may have felt somewhat inhibited in the past about expressing your sexual feelings through movement. Feeling free to move during sex can be very important in helping you let go of sexual feelings—both emotionally and physically. Additionally, exercises generally help people feel better about themselves. For instance, some people just feel more "alive"— maybe this would mean that you feel more agile or a bit more energetic as you continue to practice them. Exercise also gives a psychological boost: Possibly you will feel more in control of how your body works and feels. If you see these aspects of exercise as important for you, you may want to use the few we list here as part of a more general exercise plan for yourself. We recommend some good books for this in the Bibliography.

The following exercises are "stretchers"; basically, they are designed to help you move more freely and feel more relaxed. We all have muscles that are "tight." In some cases these muscles may reflect real feelings of tension. In other cases, these muscles have just never been used or stretched. Some of your muscles have been "asleep" or dormant for most of your adult life. Some of these exercises are common yoga positions; others are used in "body therapies" such as Bioenergetics. We offer only a few for you here. If you find that they are helpful and want to explore more exercises, a good book to have is *Total Orgasm* by Jack Lee Rosenthal, which includes these and many other exercises.

It would be best if you wore some loose-fitting clothing, or no clothing at all if you prefer. For some of the exercises, a large mirror set up against a wall or chair next to you may be helpful in order for you to see how your body moves. You may feel pretty awkward doing these exercises at first—just try not to worry about doing them perfectly. The most important thing is to try them several times and to concentrate on your physical feelings during and after the exercises. Use your own judgment about how many you do or how hard you try. Modify any that seem too strenuous and gradually work into the more difficult version. If you have had any physical problems, such as a history of back discomfort, be particularly careful to avoid those exercises that would strain troublesome muscles. If you are concerned, consult your doctor and get his or her opinion before trying these exercises.

Breathing In and Out.   Our breathing patterns change with our emotional state. For most of the early part of your sessions, you should try to maintain a full, even pattern of breathing in order to help your body stay relaxed. Start now—let your mouth remain slightly open. As you take breath into your body, let your lungs and stomach fill out. Then exhale—all the way. Pause for a natural amount of time. Then begin again. Periodically, check yourself on your breathing pattern, and make sure you are not holding your breath. Holding your breath or shallow breathing can be a sign of tension or of trying too hard, which can make it difficult for you to fully focus and enjoy physical feelings.

Chest and Neck Exercises. To help free tensions from your chest area, try this simple exercise. Lie down on your back. As you take a very deep breath, raise your arms up, then over your head in a high arch. As you exhale, put your arms back down. Repeat this five times, breathing in, (hands over head), breathing out (lowering arms). Then reverse the pairs: Breathe out as you raise your arms, breathe in as you lower them. Repeat five times. Finally, go back to the original pairing. How do you feel? What do you notice about your body?

You may feel some slight tingling in your hands and face. That's normal and good. Allow this feeling to happen—it is somewhat similar to the tingling that can occur after orgasm. Tingling is often present when we exercise our bodies; it's just that we learn to ignore it. What we want to work on is tuning into this feeling, just as you will later be tuning into feelings of sexual arousal.

Neck Tension.   Put your fingers behind your neck and feel for any muscle tension in the muscles along the ridge at the base of your skull. This area and your forehead work together to cause you discomfort—sometimes to cause headaches.

To work on this, you will need a small firm ball. Lie down on the floor, place the ball at the back of your neck, and relax your head's weight on the ball. Roll your head around to feel for tense areas. Work the ball back and forth across those areas that feel tense. Completely relax. Continue your breathing.

For your forehead, do the "spectacles stroke." Take your thumb or forefingers and stroke across your eyebrows past your temples and above your ears. Follow a pattern with your fingers that would be where glasses would be worn. Continue ten times.

The Rocking Pelvis.   This is a multipurpose exercise. As you do it you may recognize it as an intercourse thrust, or as a movement you use during your pleasuring sessions. It can be done while you are lying or sitting down. It is designed to help you loosen your lower back area and also to work on pairing deep breathing with pelvic movements. Some women have also found this exercise useful to reduce menstrual cramping.

Lie down on your back. As you breathe in, rock (rotate) your pelvis backwards by arching the small of your back; as you breathe out, let your pelvis rotate forward. Try this very slowly, holding your pelvis cocked, and then relaxing it. It may help you to have your hands on your hips as you are practicing the motion. Try it for five minutes—don't hurry, and remember to coordinate your breathing with your pelvic movements.

The Bouncing Pelvis. To make you more aware of your pelvic feelings, lie on your back, with your knees up. Raise your hips off the ground and bounce your pelvis. Try this on your stomach too, though you may want to use your hands to raise your body a little. It will help to brace your feet against the wall while you bounce.

The Pelvic Lift. A common yoga exercise, this gives you a chance to practice pelvic movements further.

Lie on your back, legs bent, knees in the air. As you take a breath, cock your pelvis backwards by arching the small of your back. Then as you expel your air, raise your pelvis slightly, one vertebra at a time, beginning at your tailbone, until it is off the ground. Continue this until you are resting on your shoulders and feet. Come back down gently and slowly. Repeat this sequence 10 times. Take your time with this. If you feel pain or discomfort, stop.

How do you feel about the exercises you've tried? You may feel discouraged that you could not do them all. Give yourself time to loosen your body in these ways. It feels awkward for most women at first. Some may have been difficult for you, others too easy. Spend a moment now and think about how you felt *during* these exercises. Did you feel good? Were you emotionally uncomfortable about any of the movements? This may be because active movements during sex may be a new experience for you, and perhaps you are unsure about how active and expressive you want to be.

If you found these exercises useful, if they make your body feel good, do them whenever it suits you. However, doing these exercises may have gotten you in touch with some uncomfortable or negative feelings you have about intercourse. For instance, you may have been reminded that certain positions during intercourse have made sex uncomfortable or unpleasant for you. Try to see these exercises as one additional way that will allow you to change the old patterns that have been unsatisfying for you in the past. They are a way of "trying out" expressive movements that can prepare you, mentally and physically, before you are actually involved in sexual activity.

SENSATE FOCUS

This procedure is to give you practice in attending to your inner bodily sensations. It will help you to deal with distracting thoughts and can also be used to help you relax and feel more in the mood for a session.

First, lie down in a comfortable, private room that is free of distractions. We're going to ask you to close your eyes and focus on sounds in the room. Really try to pick out different sounds that you're aware of. Take a few minutes now and try this before you go on.

What were some of the sounds you were able to focus on? Perhaps you noticed the sound of cars going by, the refrigerator humming, or even your own breathing. When you began to really concentrate on these sounds, you were probably less aware of other sensations, such as the feeling in your hands. This is because your awareness is like a searchlight. Focusing on one particular thing makes it clearer, while other things tend to fade into the background. As we go through this exercise, we'd like you to practice focusing your awareness on particular parts of your body. You may want to read through the directions first so that you can keep your eyes closed throughout. Or you could go through the exercise one step at a time. Reading, then focusing, then reading, and so on. If you have a tape recorder you may want to tape the procedure so all you have to do is listen. Another idea is to have someone with whom you feel comfortable read the steps to you.

Sensate Focus Exercise. Close your eyes and relax. Are you really comfortable? See if you can get more comfortable by changing your position slightly. Now become aware of your breathing. Feel the air move into your nose or mouth and down your throat into your lungs. Notice all the details of how your chest and belly move as air flows in and out of your lungs. If you notice your attention wanders to other thoughts, refocus your attention on your breathing.

Now start at your feet. Concentrate on the sensations in your toes and arches. Wiggle your toes and feet. Do they feel warm, cool, tense, loose, tingling, heavy, light? Move up to your ankles, calves, knees. Do this slowly, giving each part of your body a minute of your full inner-centered attention.

Now focus on your genitals. Are you aware of any sensations in your labia, clitoris, or vagina? Contract your vaginal muscles. Focus on the sensations this produces in your genitals.

Move to your hands. Are they tense or relaxed? Concentrate on the places where your hands and arms make contact with the floor or bed.

Move on to your shoulders, neck, and head. Try focusing your awareness on each part separately. Are you aware of any feelings of heaviness or tenseness? Does your scalp feel tight or relaxed? What smells are you aware of?

Now become aware of your breathing again. Focus on this for a few minutes. Take a few deep breaths and just enjoy the sensation of relaxing.

When you are finished, think about the following questions: 1) What was your general feeling following this exercise— relaxation, sleepiness, calm, alertness? 2) Did you find your mind wandered to other things and that you had to keep bringing your thoughts back to your body? 3) Was it more difficult to focus on your genitals than on other parts of your body?

You should try this on several different occasions before your masturbation sessions. A number of women have found that this exercise can be a good preliminary step toward getting in the mood for a session. Concentrating on the feelings in your body and shutting out the outside world for a few minutes is an important beginning for you to be able to become involved with self-pleasuring.

EROTIC LITERATURE

The previous two sections discussed ways that can help you focus on sensual and sexual feelings in your body. Reading or viewing erotic materials may also help you both to get into the mood for a session and to enhance your feelings of sexual pleasure.

Part of sexual growth is exploring different forms of sensual-sexual expression. Erotic themes are expressed in many ways, including music, art, literature, and photographs. The word "erotic" means that something sexual is suggested or depicted in the content, which in turn is likely to evoke sexual feelings in the person who is viewing or reading the material. We see erotica as a useful way to aid sexual arousal and help you to clarify for yourself what does and does not turn you on.

Like many women, you may find yourself turned on at times by erotic stories or erotic pictures in magazines. How do you feel when this happens? It would be natural for you to have mixed feelings about this. Women are often taught to ignore or at least not to admit to their sexual feelings. Recent studies of the sexuality of women have shown that some women seem to be totally unaware of their body's sexual responses. Other women may mislabel sexual arousal as either neutral feelings of genital throbbing or uncomfortable feelings of body tension. One woman going through sex therapy interpreted her nipple erection as a sign that she was cold (rather than aroused) even though it was warm 80 degree summer weather.

For a long time it was believed that women were different from men in that they were not turned on to erotica. Women were believed to be turned off by explicit sexual material, it was thought that they preferred romantic content instead. This is another myth about female sexuality that recent research has shown to be untrue. Women *do* respond to explicit sexual stories, films, and fantasies. For instance, when women hear a tape that describes two people making love, they usually become aroused regardless of the presence or absence of romantic ideas in the scene. This does not mean that romantic themes (such as a committed relationship, emotional passion, statements of mutual deep feeling and love) are not also appealing to women. It does mean that strictly erotic themes which simply describe two people who are enjoying having sex together are sexually arousing for women, just as they are for men. So if you have been turned on in the past to sexy scenes in movies or books, or if you have tried not to let yourself be aroused because you think women shouldn't be aroused, keep in mind that there is nothing wrong with you. Along the way you may have picked up feelings of guilt, embarrassment, and shame about erotic materials out of a fear of being unfeminine or too sexual. You may have even tried to avoid any exposure to erotica. Or you may have seen a few selections of sexual themes that you felt were unpleasant or distasteful (and there are plenty of sleazy selections available), and, as a result, decided that all erotica is terrible.

Not all types of erotic content are universally appealing, so don't expect yourself to become automatically aroused at the first sight of a naked body. It's fine to be selective in your tastes. What we would like to see you try to do is to view the use of erotica as an occasional enhancer of sexual pleasure, and to learn slowly to feel that using it in this way is normal and healthy. Keeping a somewhat open mind and a sense of self-exploration will help you change some of your old attitudes and discover a little more about your own sexuality.

We have included here a list of some books and magazines which has been gathered by asking other women what sort of reading has been sexually arousing to them. Although we call these "erotic," not all of them are explicitly sexual. Some, such as *The French Lieutenant's Woman* and *Tender is the Night,* are nonexplicit, suggestive, or romantic selections; while others, such as *The Godfather,* include aggression and violence as well as sex. Certain of these selections will appeal to you and others won't. Likewise, some of the pictures in the magazines may be enjoyable, others will be neutral, and others will be unpleasant for you. The majority of books, films, and magazines are directed at male customers (since traditionally men are the ones who buy them), so you will probably have to hunt around a while to find something that appeals to you. Many of these books are advertised in magazines, or are easily found in bookstores and even in some supermarkets. Others may have to be ordered for you or purchased in an adult bookstore. These stores are fairly common today; and women, though less frequently than men, do go in to shop around. If you feel comfortable about going into one, you may want to consider it. If not, there are lots of choices available through other sources.

BOOKS

Boys and Girls Together by William Goldman
Candy by Maxwell Kenton
The Carpetbaggers by Harold Robbins
Couples by John Updike
Diary of Anais Nin by Anais Nin
Doctor Zhivago by Boris Pasternak
Fanny Hill by John Cleland
Flowers of Evil by Charles Baudelaire
Forbidden Flowers by Nancy Friday
The Fountainhead by Ayn Rand
The Four-Gated City by Doris Lessing
The Fox by D.H. Lawrence
The French Lieutenant's Woman by John Fowles
The Godfather by Mario Puzo

The Group by Mary McCarthy
The Happy Hooker by Xaviera Hollander
The Joy of Sex by Alex Comfort
The Kama Sutra by Vatsayana
Lady Chatterley's Lover by D.H. Lawrence
Love Poems by Anne Sexton
Madame Bovary by Gustave Flaubert
More Joy by Alex Comfort
My Life and Loves by Frank Harris
My Secret Garden by Nancy Friday
Myra Breckinridge by Gore Vidal
The Pearl by Anonymous
The Perfumed Garden of the Sheikh Nefzaoui by Anonymous
Peyton Place by Grace Metalious
Romeo and Juliet by William Shakespeare
The Sensuous Couple by Robert Chartham
The Sensuous Woman by "J"
Sons and Lovers by D.H. Lawrence
The Story of O by Pauline Reage
Tender is the Night by F. Scott Fitzgerald
Tropic of Cancer by Henry Miller
Valley of the Dolls by Jacqueline Susanne
The Virgin and the Gypsy by D.H. Lawrence
Women in Love by D.H. Lawrence

MAGAZINES

Penthouse Forum
Penthouse
Playboy
Playgirl
Viva

Your Sessions.   Try spending 30–45 minutes in your pleasuring sessions at least three times a week. Use erotic literature or look through a magazine that has pictures that are sexually

interesting for you. You can begin stimulating yourself as you read or look, or wait until you either feel some good feelings (for instance throbbing or tingling) in your genitals or just feel like touching yourself. If you find what you are looking at is distracting from your pleasure, put it down and focus all your attention on your physical sensations.

Something else that might happen is that you might read a passage during an early part of the day, but not get turned on until you think about it later. At that time, find a place where you can have privacy and try stimulating yourself.

Again, erotica is an enhancer. Try using it a few times and if you enjoy it, continue as often as you like. You may be concerned that you will come to like or depend on this too much. Try seeing this as something special you are doing for yourself right now. In the course of learning what arouses you, you may want to read from an erotic book or look at erotic pictures more frequently now than you will later. That's fine. This is still an exploration of feelings and experiences.

FANTASY

Something else which can help you focus on your body and its sensations is fantasy. At times, you may find your body is not responding to stimulation because your mind is elsewhere. Your mind may "wander," or you may find that you are distracted by stray thoughts. As we said before, sexual pleasure means involving your body *and* your mind. Fantasy is one way to do this.

All of us have fantasized at times. We may be sitting and reading, or in the middle of working, when all of a sudden we realize that our mind has wandered off and we are day dreaming. Dreams and "day dreams" are a form of fantasy. The difference is that when we are dreaming we have little conscious control over the content of our dreams, but when we "day dream," we have the pleasurable opportunity to create or recreate a scene consciously.

How do you feel when you think about fantasizing something sexual? Is it something you find easy or difficult to do, or is it something you have never deliberately tried? Some women find it easier to fantasize than others, but it is something you can teach yourself to do. Like becoming comfortable with sexual feelings, it means becoming comfortable enough with sexual thoughts to really "let go." This means you must feel basically good about yourself and be willing to trust yourself.

Sometimes, we may be afraid of *what* we fantasize. What will it mean if we fantasize about someone other than our spouse or partner, or if we fantasize about something that we wouldn't really enjoy or act out in real life? You may feel (or perhaps you have been taught) that to think about doing something is as bad as doing it. If you have these fears, it may help you to cope with them if you realize that sexual fantasy is a normal, natural activity that many men and women do more or less throughout their lives. Fantasizing about something does not mean that you will actually do it. In fact, the beauty of fantasy is that it allows you the freedom to experiment with sexual variety beyond the limits of reality.

If your fantasies involve doing something sexual with another woman, this does not automatically mean that you secretly prefer women as sexual partners. Or if your fantasy themes include orgies, or the idea of another person forcing you to do something sexual (while you are tied up, for example), it does not mean that there is something wrong with you. Such fantasies are quite common among women, and enjoying them does not mean that you are immature, perverted, or that you would necessarily act them out if a real situation presented itself. Rather, fantasies serve many purposes. They are a way of re-experiencing pleasurable or exciting situations, behaviors, and experiences; expressing creativity; and satisfying natural desires for variety, novelty, and excitement.

We'd like you to get a copy of *My Secret Garden* or *Forbidden Flowers* by Nancy Friday (in paperback for under $2.00). These are collections of women's fantasies. You will probably experience lots of different reactions as you read them. Some fantasies will surprise you, some will make you laugh, some will turn you on, and some will definitely turn you off. What we would like you to get from reading these books is a feeling for the tremendous range of fantasies. We hope that you will feel more comfortable about exploring your own fantasies, and about seeing how they develop and change over time.

Because these are women's fantasies, they have a special meaning for you. If you have a male partner, you may want to have him read the books; but don't be surprised if his reactions are different from your own. Sharing can be a good experience if you don't judge, evaluate, or impose expectations on each other (more on this in Chapters 8–10). On the other hand, you may not feel like sharing your fantasies or reactions to these fantasies with your partner. That's all right, too. You can have your own private fantasy—your own "Secret Garden."

For the rest of the program, we'd like you to try to develop and use fantasy each time you have a self-pleasuring session. After you've relaxed and made yourself comfortable, play around with some ideas that might be appealing fantasies.

If you currently have a sexual partner, you might try imagining him in a fantasy. Close your eyes and pretend that he is touching your body as you touch yourself. Imagine that he is caressing all of the favorite places on your body, and that he is willing to pleasure you in any way you want. Let your imagination go.

Or you might like fantasizing about an actual occasion on which you made love with someone. Let your mind take you back—linger over the sexually pleasant things you and he did. It may help to recall as many details as possible: Where you were, how you got undressed or whether your clothes were partially on, what he or you said, what his skin and hair felt like, how you both moved, and so forth.

There are several very common fantasy themes that women enjoy. One theme is that of being forced to have sex with someone. The idea of force may be expressed in many ways. Sometimes the force theme does not include any cooperation on the woman's part; for instance, some women imagine that they are being raped. The force theme can also incorporate some cooperation on the woman's part. An example of this would be a scene in which a woman is sitting in a restaurant: A man approaches her, they are attracted to each other, they talk, they walk to a place where they are alone, and the man becomes sexually forceful.

Why is the idea of force appealing to a lot of women? No one really knows, but there are a number of possibilities. One is that women are given conflicting messages about being sexual. They are generally taught the importance of being sexually attractive, but they are also taught that they should, at some point, say "no." In other words, women should look sexual but not really *be* sexual. Fantasy provides a good solution to this dilemma; the woman who is forced into sex has very little if any choice and responsibility for what happens. Being forced helps eliminate feelings of guilt about being sexual and aggressive.

Another speculation regarding the popularity of the force theme is that being "taken" sexually assumes that the woman is desirable. The cultural message for both male and female sexuality is that being desirable and sexually irresistible are very important. Force might indirectly imply that the female is so utterly sexually appealing that the man cannot control himself. (Of course, being irresistible does not have to mean that force must be involved—you may imagine yourself tantalizing or stimulating several men where *you* are in control of what happens.)

Another common theme incorporates more "romantic" elements into a sexual scene. Often women imagine themselves having a clandestine affair with an important or well-known person. The fantasized person might be someone you know or someone you have seen on the stage or in films. Imagining that you are making love with someone you have seen in the movies may be particularly easy, since the majority of movies include some sexual activity.

Another theme that many women find arousing is that of being aggressive. You may find that you like to imagine yourself in control of a sexual encounter, selecting a partner of your choice, initiating sexual activity with him, turning him on, teasing him to the point of orgasm several times before you let him climax, having him moaning for more, being able to have him do anything you want him to do. You can expand this to several different men, each of whom you control according to your sexual desires. Aggression in fantasy allows women a chance to express what is not culturally approved of: the initiation and direction (or even domination) of a sexual encounter.

In your own attempts at developing fantasies, you might start by recalling a film scene that you particularly liked and add your own preferences. Or, if it suits you better, you might begin your self-pleasuring session by reading about someone else's fantasy from *My Secret Garden,* by reading parts of an erotic story, or perhaps by looking at some pictures that you find sexually appealing. As you get more into the fantasy, and can picture it clearly, begin touching yourself. At some point you can put the book down and continue the fantasy on your own.

SUGGESTIONS TO EXPAND YOUR ABILITY TO FANTASIZE

1. A fantasy does not have to be some elaborate and involved story. Your fantasy may just be a series of brief images (a particular scene, a look, a face, a touch) that holds meaning for you.

2. What turns you on can be something that is not explicitly sexual. It may be more romantic and sensual—such as the thought of someone stroking your face tenderly, someone holding you very close, or being surprised by someone's touch.

3. Little details can often be important to the creation of a fantasy. Try to discover what elements are important to you. A few ideas along these lines come from other women who have described what parts of their fantasies are arousing: The thought of their partner getting very aroused while they are making love; the image of their partner reaching orgasm; the thought that

their partner will do anything for any length of time to give them pleasure (such as 30 minutes of oral genital stimulation or an hour of intercourse); pretending to have sex in a different place—in the woods, underwater, in the snow, on a beach; or spontaneous sex, such as having sex the minute you walk in the door without even taking off any clothes (you can make this fun by keeping some of your clothes on while stimulating yourself.)

4. Also, try blending your sensate focus exercises with a fantasy. For instance, as you concentrate on the feelings in your thighs, touch yourself there and imagine that your fantasy partner's hands are doing the caressing.

After you've tried some of the above a few times, you will probably find it easier and more enjoyable to fantasize during your pleasure sessions.

BEFORE YOU GO ON

Try to have five or sex sessions over the next two weeks in which you use fantasy, erotic literature, sensate focus and loosening exercises as part of your sessions. You can try one or two of these focus techniques during each session, and begin to get an idea of which ones seem to be the most useful for you.

6

Going Further

At this point in the program you've been masturbating for up to 30 minutes. Although you've probably experienced high arousal you haven't yet been able to have an orgasm. Don't panic! You've learned a lot about your body and how it responds—you just need some more time and exploration. Let's make sure, however, that other problems or feelings aren't interfering.

1. *Do you find it difficult to get in the mood for your sessions? Do you sometimes feel that you would rather not spend this time with yourself?* Most women experience feelings like these at times; but if you find this happening frequently, you need to stop and think about what may be causing this. Think about the difference between those times when you enjoy feeling sensual or sexual and when you don't. Does the kind of day you had make a difference? This often affects how we

interact with others and feel about ourselves. If you've had a hectic day, been under pressure, or had conflicts with others, it's not surprising that you may have trouble focusing on yourself in pleasurable ways. Putting off your session for another day is one possibility. Or you might try allowing yourself some extra time to unwind. Try to set aside some time for yourself in the evening—a time when you can be alone if you want, and a time when you can relax. A bath, a small drink, reading, or running through the relaxation exercise—any or all may help you to put the day behind you.

2. *How does the time at which you do your sessions influence their quality?* If you are putting your sessions off till the end of the day, you may feel physically or mentally worn out. You may come to feel that your sessions are just one more thing you have to do before you can relax. If you begin your sessions in this frame of mind, nothing you do will give you much pleasure. Instead, you may pressure yourself to hurry up and end the session, and you may feel guilty and blame yourself afterwards.

If this seems to be causing you problems, try changing the time at which you have your sessions. Perhaps during the day, if you're home alone for a while, or in the early evening, if you can arrange to be free of responsibilities for an hour or so. Mornings can also be nice times for pleasuring yourself, so try to arrange to have a morning or two free to see if this is a better time for you.

3. *Are your good sessions more likely to happen when you feel good about yourself?* Feeling positive about yourself probably makes it easier for you to deal with any reservations you may have about taking time for yourself, and about masturbating. It's easier to feel that you deserve the time, and that you have a right to spend it on yourself.

When you feel badly about yourself though, things tend to look bleak. You may think about all the other things you should be doing, or about why you feel badly about yourself, and old doubts about yourself and sex may intrude.

Unfortunately, most of us, throughout our lives, are involved in struggles to feel better about ourselves. We have a tendency to compare ourselves with others as a way of judging our own worth. The most obvious example of this is the concerns most women have about physical appearance. But there are many other areas in which we can feel that our expectations for ourselves are not being met—for example, in our jobs or in our efforts at being a good parent. It may be difficult for you to accept yourself. You may be more critical of yourself than anyone else. Do you have an "inner voice" that is always saying, "Don't do or think this," or "You shouldn't?" or "How could you?" Most of us carry around some inner critics, since we all have some parts of ourselves that we would like to change or improve. But if you *never* seem to measure up to your expectations, you need to re-evaluate them and also to learn how to go about feeling better about yourself. In the Bibliography at the back of the book, we have listed some books which others have found helpful. If self-criticism is causing you a great deal of concern at this point in your life, that can make it hard for you to really let yourself get involved in your sessions.

4. *Something else which may be interfering with your sessions may be feelings about taking time just for yourself.* You may rush through your sessions because you feel guilty that you are being selfish and taking time away from your family or from other responsibilities.

Perhaps you don't feel justified in taking time for yourself because you are just far more accustomed to giving time to others. This is true for most women. We are brought up with the idea that being a good person means doing things for other people, and that the satisfaction of our family, friends, spouse, and children, is far more important than our own satisfaction. And yet, at times, we all feel the need to explore some things that are pleasing to *us,* as part of our desire for fulfillment and self-expression. These things contribute to our growing sense of identity as women and as individuals which, if not given a chance to develop, are likely to breed feelings of resentment. If you are doing some things for yourself, the time you spend with others is likely to be more enjoyable and rewarding.

What does this mean for you? Your sexual expression is obviously a part of your identity, and you need and deserve the time to develop it. If you don't feel that you can take or that you deserve the time, what sorts of reasons are you giving yourself—are you over-committed to serving other people? Does it just seem uncomfortable? Try rethinking your reasons in the light of what your own priorities for growth and change really are. It may be that you have to occasionally remind yourself that you do deserve some time to yourself in order to develop (sexually and otherwise) into the person you want to be.

Perhaps you're uncomfortable about taking time for your individual sessions because you feel that your partner, or spouse, or children, resents this time you spend alone. If you have children and they are old enough, they can understand the need for privacy and for some time alone. They do not have to know how you are spending this time. You may be reading or just resting, taking a relaxing bath or having a pleasuring session. See if you can arrange some time for yourself during the day a few times a week when the children will respect your need to be alone.

If you feel your spouse or partner is uncomfortable about your individual sessions, try talking this over with him. See if you can understand his fears and concerns and offer some reassurance. These individual sessions are important to both of you, since what you are learning will help improve sex with your partner.

Perhaps one concern may be that enjoying masturbation will turn you off to sex with your partner. Actually, masturbation does not decrease the desire for sex with another person. In fact, as we said earlier, women who are orgasmic through masturbation are more likely to be orgasmic with a partner. Learning to enjoy sensual and sexual feelings, then, will make sex with another person more enjoyable. Most women describe the experience of orgasm during masturbation as different from orgasm while making love with a partner. Both are enjoyable, but, at the same time, each is different. Becoming orgasmic through masturbation can enrich the quality of the sexual relationship you develop with your partner.

5. *How you feel about a session before you start also influences what happens. Are you aware of any particular feelings you have before a session? Do you look forward to it, or do you feel some reluctance—a desire to get it over with?* Feeling some reluctance is not unusual at this stage of sexual growth. Earlier in the book, we mentioned that part of you is probably somewhat unsure of what becoming orgasmic will be like and of what changes it will bring. You may be afraid that becoming orgasmic will cause you to "lose control" over yourself. You may see orgasm as something powerful which you may feel you can't control. In letting go and really experiencing your sexual feelings, you may be afraid that they will overwhelm you or that you will be giving some power or control over yourself to someone else.

Since most of us have been taught as children to "control" ourselves (especially in terms of anything to do with sex), it is hard for us to think about letting any of our strong emotions out. Were you ever told, as a child: "Don't cry," "Sit still," "Act like an adult," "Don't be so childish"? All these reminders, in various ways, gave us the message: "Control yourself!" After so many years of overcontrol, it makes sense that we feel out of touch with our emotions or feelings, come to see them as shameful or dangerous, and so ignore or deny them. A good example is the fear many people have of expressing anything negative. If we've been told as children: "Don't say that" or "That's horrible!" or "How could you say that to your mother, father, brother!" we begin to see our feelings, particularly negative feelings, as powerful weapons.

Women describe this fear in relation to sex in many ways. Perhaps you've felt yourself stopping when you get to a certain point of arousal. Are you aware of almost telling yourself to cool down? One woman described the feeling as one of being on the edge of a cliff. If she let herself get any more aroused, she would fall off.

The first step in overcoming these fears is to learn to trust yourself. Perhaps you've noticed that in becoming aroused, there are changes in your body—for example, increased muscle tension, heavier breathing, a desire for continued movements of your hips—that may seem to "take over." As orgasm approaches, these changes intensify, as does the desire to continue stimulation. It can feel as if your physical desire is overcoming you. Orgasm does involve uncontrollable physical responses, but not all women show their reactions in the same way. Some women merely sigh and shudder a bit during orgasm, other women moan or cry out, and throw their bodies around, and still other women let their bodies become rigid with sexual tension. Even for a particular woman, expressiveness during orgasm varies from orgasm to orgasm. The next exercise is designed to help you deal with some fears you might have about your own expression of orgasm. *We'd like you to try this even if you feel that you don't experience these particular fears at this time.*

ROLE-PLAYING ORGASM

We call this exercise *Role-Playing Orgasm.* What we'd like you to do is to dream up a fantasy of a "wild" orgasm and act it out.

Set aside 30 minutes to one hour. Begin one of your self-pleasuring sessions in the usual way. The first time, begin role-playing orgasm after you've pleasured yourself for a while but *before* you become extremely aroused. Move around, tense your muscles, lie very rigid, do some pelvic rocking, make noises—do whatever seems really extreme to you. Moan, scratch, pummel the bed, cry—the more exaggerated the better. Stop pleasuring yourself if you want, or continue while you have your "orgasm." You will probably feel awkward doing this the first few times but it will become easier with practice. Remember, the way you act is not really the way you would or should act. For this exercise pretend to be the star in your own orgasmic fantasy! Try this exercise two or three times over the next week (at least once during each individual session you have). By the end of the week we expect you will be bored by this exercise, but a little surer of yourself. You also may have discovered some ways in which you were afraid to let go—movements or feelings you were afraid to let happen. After you've tried this exercise, answer these questions for yourself.

Were you aware of any thoughts or feelings that disturbed you about doing this exercise? Perhaps you associate being orgasmic with being promiscuous. When you think about being sexually responsive and uninhibited what comes to your mind? Are you afraid that tremendous changes will take place in your life? That you will constantly think about sex or that you will want sex all the time? These fears come from early experiences which taught us that sex was bad and that sexual feelings could easily get out of control. To be sexual often meant to be secretive and to feel guilty. While growing up, most of us were probably warned against getting involved sexually with boys, and we were taught to worry about our reputations and loss of self-respect. Being a sexual person became associated with being "loose" or "promiscuous," with being a person whom others would not respect. Not being sexual became associated with being a good girl, someone whom others would respect and value.

You are not a girl any more, but you may still feel some conflicts about "growing up" sexually. Given the kind of upbringing most of us experienced, it's natural to feel somewhat ambivalent about making changes. You're probably worried on some level about how you'll feel about yourself, about how your partner will feel about you, and about how others will see you. Perhaps it will help if you look back on your years of growing up and dating and realize that the way you felt about sex then does not have to be the way you feel about it now. How many of us have said, "I will do this differently with my own life, husband, children, job, friend," and so on? We learn from the experiences of our parents and peers; and as adults, we can choose to keep or discard various practices, attitudes, or beliefs that we grew up with as we learn to see them differently. It is possible to decide for yourself how you want to feel about sex as an adult. If you want to see sex and your own sexuality as something positive, something that makes you feel good about yourself, you can learn to feel this way. The things you have been doing as part of this book will help. Give yourself a chance to change.

YOUR PHYSICAL RESPONSES

Even though you've made a lot of progress in learning about your body, you may still be feeling somewhat anxious about having your first orgasm. Will you be able to have one? When will it happen? What will it feel like?

Being concerned about orgasm is natural at this stage; but worrying about it and "trying too hard" are the very things which may keep you from experiencing one. Worry and anxiety interfere with your body's natural responses, and will distract you from focusing on sensations of pleasure and arousal. Orgasm is actually a reflex that occurs automatically if your body is stimulated long enough, and in the ways which work for you. However, just as you can sometimes stop yourself from sneezing or coughing, it is possible for you to make it hard for orgasm to occur. At times you may find that you are so concerned about whether or not you will experience orgasm that you take a "spectator role." At these times you will be aware of "watching" yourself for any sign of arousal, and of course the more you "watch" the less likely it is that you will become aroused. The best thing to do at these times is to refocus your attention onto what you are feeling; in other words, try to get back in touch with your body and what it's telling you. The sensate focusing exercises in the previous chapter will help you to do this. Remember that you will experience orgasm when there is no pressure on you to have one. You can't will yourself to have one, just as a man can't will himself to have an erection. What you are learning now are ways to "let" your body experience orgasm. It's just a matter of time.

Thinking about experiencing orgasm has probably made you more aware of some of your concerns; but again, it is normal for you to be somewhat anxious about this experience. Most of us have no idea what to expect, except what we read in popular magazines, books, or movies. Unfortunately, these are sometimes poor sources of accurate information. We feel that it's important for you to have some understanding of how your body responds to stimulation and arousal. The phases of sexual response that are described below are based on Master's and Johnson's research on human sexuality. You've probably already noticed some of the responses we're going to discuss; however, many changes take place inside of your where you can't see them.

Look at the drawing of the female genitals before arousal. In

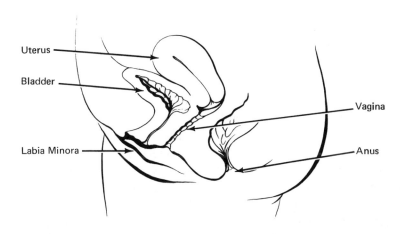

UNAROUSED PHASE

this state, the vagina is not an open space. Rather, the walls of the vagina almost touch each other. These walls are incredibly elastic and mold themselves to accommodate the erect penis. For this reason, there is really no such thing as a vagina or penis that is "too small" or "too big."

The first phase of sexual response (the *excitement phase)* begins when you experience some erotic feelings. This triggers the walls of the vagina to secrete droplets of moisture called vaginal lubrication. The amount of lubrication you have depends on a number of things.

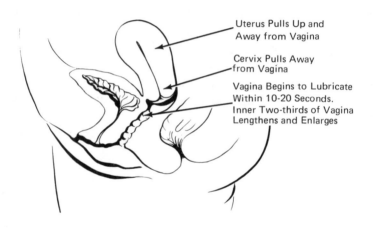

Uterus Pulls Up and
Away from Vagina

Cervix Pulls Away
from Vagina

Vagina Begins to Lubricate
Within 10-20 Seconds.
Inner Two-thirds of Vagina
Lengthens and Enlarges

EXCITEMENT PHASE

Certain contraceptive pills may increase or decrease your natural lubrication. Pregnancy and aging also affect it. Since the vagina is a warm, moist place, bacteria and other oganisms can grow within it. The natural acidity of the vagina usually controls this growth. However, at times infections can occur which can cause discomfort and also increase your vaginal secretions. Some of the signs of vaginal infection are itching or soreness, excessive lubrication and discharge, and unusual or disagreeable odor. Vaginal infections are becoming more common and can be difficult, at times, to control completely. One reason for this is that oral contraceptives tend to make vaginal infections more likely. Also, antibiotics, which may be prescribed for you to treat an infection in another part of your body, destroy the natural balance of organisms in your vagina, allowing some to take control. If you are aware of any discomfort or of a noticeable change in the amount, texture, or odor of your discharge, you should check with your doctor.

Along with these differences in lubrication, there is a wide range of *normal* variability. If penetration and intercourse is something uncomfortable for you, try using a lubricating gel or cream. You need not feel embarrassed about using a vaginal lubricant during sex. This does not mean that you are abnormal, "frigid," unexcited, or that you and your partner are doing something wrong. Many women put a little lubricant on their genitals or their partner's penis *each* time they have intercourse. Then, instead of worrying about how well they're lubricated, they're free to really enjoy and get into what they're feeling.

You may experience this first phase of sexual repsonse as a feeling of tightness or fullness in your genitals. This is because your genitals are filling with blood. This causes your labia to swell and your clitoris to become firmer or erect, just as a man's penis does. The clitoris may feel larger when you touch it and the clitoral shaft feels firm. You may be aware of some lubrication or moisture seeping out of your vagina, although do not be alarmed if it doesn't. Not all women who lubricate well are aware when they're lubricated. If you continue genital touching you'll probably (if you haven't already) notice that the clitoris seems to disappear. This is because as you become aroused the clitoris retracts or hides under the hood of the shaft. Don't worry that you've lost it! This happens *automatically* because the clitoris becomes extremely sensitive to touch once you're aroused. In its new position, it is still very sensitive and this retraction does not lessen arousal.

You may also notice changes in your breasts at this time. Your nipples may become erect or your breasts may appear to swell. Some women experience extreme sensitivity of their breasts during this phase and enjoy only very gentle touching. This sensitivity sometimes decreases as they become more aroused, but most women have definite preferences on how they like their breasts to be touched.

In addition to these changes that may be visible, there are changes going on inside your body. During the excitement phase, your uterus enlarges and rises up from its "resting" position. The vagina enlarges and "balloons," allowing it to accommodate the penis during intercourse.

During the second phase (The Plateau Phase), you may be aware of some "blotching" or reddish areas on your skin. This is due to changes in your blood flow during arousal, and it may or may not occur. It is particularly noticeable in both men and women with fair skin. You may notice your breathing and heart rate becoming more rapid. The color of your labia minora or "inner lips" darkens, and the uterus completes its change in position while the vagina is widely "ballooned."

During this time you may experience feelings of tension or

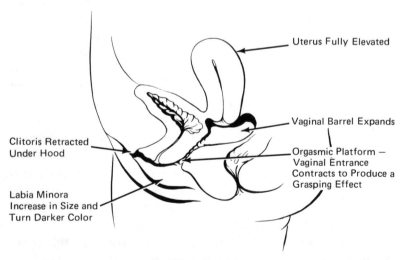

Uterus Fully Elevated

Vaginal Barrel Expands

Orgasmic Platform — Vaginal Entrance Contracts to Produce a Grasping Effect

Clitoris Retracted Under Hood

Labia Minora Increase in Size and Turn Darker Color

PLATEAU PHASE

heaviness in your genitals, legs, stomach, or arms. Often these sensations are neither pleasant or unpleasant. If you are not used to feelings of arousal, you may experience these feelings as somewhat scary or uncomfortable. You may feel your body is "running away with you" and that you are out of control. These are normal feelings. Over time, you will learn to relax and trust your body. As you become comfortable with the feelings and emotions of arousal, you'll find yourself tuning in to them more and enjoying your body's responsiveness. This phase usually leads to the next phase, where orgasm occurs. However, sometimes you may experience feelings of high arousal without orgasm occurring. This is not necessarily a problem, unless it happens frequently. Illness, drugs, and alcohol can affect how you respond. Sometimes you may not feel the desire to go on to orgasm. Having a close, loving, sharing experience with your partner may be all you desire at times. Men also, as they mature, experience less of a need for orgasm and ejaculation on each sexual occasion.

However, perhaps you are *only* able to reach this plateau phase and have never experienced orgasm. You probably have felt very frustrated and physically uncomfortable from a lack of orgasmic release. Over a period of time when you've met with repeated frustration you've learned to "turn yourself off" at the first sign of arousal. The physical signs of arousal (tension, and so on) probably feel uncomfortable, and make you anxious and worried about how well you'll do this time. Through these chapters, you'll get a chance to experience these feelings of arousal and hopefully begin to enjoy them as signs of your body's responsiveness to pleasure.

The Orgasmic Phase brings a series of rhythmical contractions to the muscles around your vagina and to the uterus itself. You may be aware of these contractions or you may not, depending on what is your particular pattern.

During orgasm you may respond in different ways. However, it's good to remember that the way you respond to stimulation and orgasm at a particular time may not be the way in which

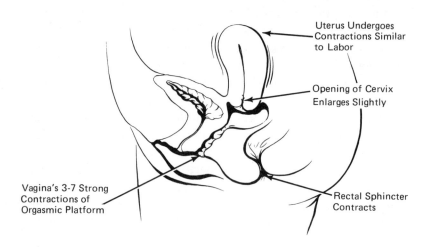

Uterus Undergoes
Contractions Similar
to Labor

Opening of Cervix
Enlarges Slightly

Vagina's 3-7 Strong
Contractions of
Orgasmic Platform

Rectal Sphincter
Contracts

ORGASMIC PHASE

you respond the next time. What's important is to "let go" and enjoy the experience. Feeling good about yourself as a person means feeling free enough to do what you enjoy at the time.

You may feel like moving your body around during orgasm or you may prefer to be absolutely still and really focus in on your feelings. You may find yourself making some noise, wanting to cry, using erotic words. You may be afraid that if you really let go, you will grimace and appear ugly, urinate, or turn your partner off. Whatever your concerns are, they're probably interfering with the enjoyment you get from your body at *all* phases of the sexual cycle. If you have a set of rules or a rigid set of expectations about sex, you're bound to lose out on the spontaneity, fun, and sense of excitement that sexual exploration can provide.

It is not necessary for an erect penis to be in the vagina in order for a women to experience orgasm. Orgasm results from a build-up of body tension through direct or indirect stimulation of the glans of the clitoris. During intercourse, the in and out motion of the penis in the vagina pulls on the labia. This causes friction between the hood and the clitoris itself. Other feelings —from the breasts (if they're being touched), from the inside of the vagina, such as the penis bumping the cervix and from stimulation to the first third of the vagina—adds to this buildup of body tension and excitement. However, enough stimulation for orgasm can occur in other ways. A few women are able to experience orgasm through having intense breast stimulation only. Stimulation of the clitoris through self-pleasuring or a partner's touch can also produce orgasm. Oral-genital stimulation, the use of an electric vibrator, directing a stream of water onto your genitals—all these ways can produce orgasm for different women.

Some women find it difficult or impossible to reach orgasm during intercourse, although they may be able to through other forms of stimulation. Sometimes orgasm through intercourse will develop over a time when a couple has become familiar with each other's sexual responsiveness and preferences. However, some women never experience orgasm through intercourse alone. This is probably because the particular way they "fit" together with their partner just doesn't provide enough clitoral stimulation to result in orgasm. The addition of some direct clitoral touching (with finger or vibrator) during intercourse usually makes orgasm possible.

After orgasm your body gradually returns to its unaroused state. Enlargement of the breasts, clitoris and labia diminishes. Heart rate becomes slower. The uterus descends and the vagina returns to its unaroused size and shape. Sex flush and changes in the color of the labia fade.

Some women have found that stimulation during the time almost immediately after the first orgasm, results in a second orgasm (or even more). This is called multiple orgasm. Not all women enjoy being restimulated shortly after orgasm or find that they are able to reach a second peak of arousal. When you become orgasmic, let your body be your guide.

ORGASM "TRIGGERS"

By now you've learned to understand your body a little better. At the times when you feel that everything cooperates to make for a fine session, you feel pretty good about yourself and you're in a good mood. You find it easier to fantasize and get into and focus on what you're doing with your body. You feel in control of how things are going and of how you're responding. You are probably aware of feelings of increasing arousal, but for some reason you don't seem to be able to have an orgasm.

At times like these it's possible to help nature's rhythm along a bit and give yourself that little extra nudge that your body seems to need. Below, we've listed some suggestions that we've learned from other women. Not all of these will be right for you. Again, let your body be your guide.

1. During sexual arousal, try deliberately tensing your legs, stomach, arms, or feet or exaggerating these things if you find yourself doing them. Body tension (such as pointing your toes or clenching your hands) is sometimes an automatic response, and increasing this tension often triggers orgasm.

2. Do some vaginal muscle contractions or Kegels. The squeeze and release movements often enhance arousal and will keep you focused on your genital sensations.

3. As you get aroused, change position so that your head is hanging back over the edge of the bed or couch. This increases blood flow to your head and changes your breathing, both of which seem to add to feelings of tension and arousal in some women.

4. Try really letting go. Begin to role-play an orgasm. Move your hips. Say some exciting words to yourself as though you were encouraging your body—"come" or "more"—whatever seems right to you at the time.

5. When you feel some arousal, try teasing yourself. Move away from the area you're concentrating on and then come back to it. Move your fingers over your breasts, nipples, and stomach as well as your clitoris. Or change the pressure of your touch or your tempo as you touch your clitoris.

6. You might try arranging a mirror so that you can watch while you're pleasuring yourself.

7. Read a favorite passage from an erotic book after you've spent some time stimulating yourself. Or try really imagining yourself *in* your most intense fantasy. Really get into it. Let yourself go.

8. Pick a sensual or sexy nightgown, bra, slip, or underpants. Begin your session with this on. Feel the texture of this with your fingers. How does it feel to touch your breasts or genitals through this material? Undress yourself after a while or continue partially dressed if you like the feeling.

9. Try touching yourself in a different position. If you've always pleasured yourself while on your back, turn over. You might try just having your rear up and your head and chest resting on a pillow. Or lie on your side or on your back with your legs up if you've always kept them stretched out flat. Try some body movements, such as moving your pelvis in the way that you did during the pelvic exercises you've practiced.

10. Try holding your breath for a short while or breathing heavily (panting).

How do you feel after reading this list? If you feel enthused and want to rush and try all of them at once, remember that these suggestions are only a small part of what you do. They aren't magic. Doing these when you're not in the mood for sex, when you're distracted or tired, won't bring on an instant orgasm. Spending time on yourself, creating a sensual environment, and enjoying your body are essential for responsiveness. So, choose one or two things to try from our list that sound good to you. Give yourself at least three sessions to explore the possibilities you decide to try.

If you're feeling a little anxious or overwhelmed after reading our list, it's probably because you're still worried about how well you'll do. You may be thinking: "If some or all of these don't work for me, then there must be something *wrong* with me." These kinds of worries are bound to interfere with your pleasure. If you do find yourself worrying about your progress, thats okay; it's natural. As you continue to practice focusing and triggers you will slowly get more comfortable and notice some progress. Some things will not work, but with time you will be able to discover what does work for you.

Sometimes, just increasing the time you spend stimulating yourself will bring about orgasm. For this reason, we're going to have you spend 30–45 minutes pleasuring yourself during your sessions. The way you approach this time is very important. If you feel discouraged because it seems to be taking you so long to get aroused or to reach orgasm, try to be patient with yourself. It will not take as long later on. Earlier we mentioned that having one orgasm makes it easier and more likely that you'll have another. The more orgasms you have, the less time it will take you to feel arousal. Right now is your chance to really give yourself the time you need. You have no one else's needs or desires to consider but your own. You deserve this time. Remember, you're making up for years of being out of touch with your body and its responsiveness.

DURING YOUR SESSIONS

This week we'd like you to keep the things we have discussed in this chapter in mind. Your self-pleasuring sessions should last 30–45 minutes. Try role-playing orgasm and try some orgasm triggers when you feel yourself getting aroused. Fantasize and focus in on the good feelings your body is giving you. After you have had two self-pleasuring sessions in this way, answer these questions for yourself. 1) How did you feel about these sessions? 2) Are you finding it easier to fantasize and let go, or are you running away or turning off when you experience arousal? If so, practice the fantasy exercise (Chapter 5), role-playing orgasm exercise (Chapter 6), and the sensate focus exercises (Chapter 5), again. Think of some ways you can distract yourself when you notice you are turning off. Fantasy, erotic pictures, stories, music, or even thinking of a pleasant scene while continuing to pleasure yourself may help.

If you have had orgasms, enjoy them! Continue with your individual sessions so that you can explore this new experience further. When you feel ready, move on to Chapter 7.

If you have not had an orgasm, try not to focus on this in your sessions. Keep trying this step, if you feel that it is beginning to work for you, at least four to six times over the next two weeks. It's not unusual for it to take two to three weeks or more at this stage before orgasm may occur. If you feel that you are getting close to orgasm, and if you are highly aroused during your sessions, you may just need some more time. You are not doing anything wrong, and you haven't failed. You may just be one of the many women who need additional stimulation. If, after two to three weeks or so, you have not had an orgasm, you are ready to move on to Chapter 7.

7

Using a Vibrator: A Little Help from a Friend

How did today begin for you? Let us be a little presumptuous for a moment and sketch what might have happened: The alarm rings, you shut it off. Back to bed for a quick second snooze, then up again, walk to the bathroom, turn on a light, and take a quick shower. Then you're off to the kitchen to plug in the coffee pot or put bread in the toaster. While the coffee is on, you are blowing your hair dry with a hair dryer. After breakfast, you quickly iron a blouse. Moments later, you rush to your car and then go on to work or to run errands.

Well, perhaps some of this sounds familiar. It takes a moment to realize how much we depend upon some electrical devices to enhance or maintain the quality of our lives. Most of us take these things pretty much for granted. With the exception of wasteful uses of energy, we usually don't question the fact that such devices are generally helpful additions to our lives, and that using them is okay. We don't, for instance, assume that people are lazy if they prefer electric to hand wound alarm clocks. Nor do we worry about a car becoming a "crutch" for someone who lives four miles from work, because they *should really* walk.

However, many people feel differently when it comes to the area of sex. In this next phase of your personal growth program, we'd like you to feel comfortable enough to explore vibrators as another means of learning about yourself.

How do you feel about the idea of using an electric vibrator during your individual self-stimulation sessions? Perhaps you feel you shouldn't need to—that it's not natural—or you may have fears that a vibrator will become a sexual crutch and that you will become dependent on it forever—that you will not be able to get sexual pleasure in any other way.

If you see the use of a vibrator as unnatural, perhaps you can try thinking about it as an extension of yourself that can help you with your sexual response. It really only provides another way for you to explore your sexuality. Often our ideas of what is natural and right in sex come from things we learned to feel when we were younger. Perhaps you've already changed some of your ideas just by progressing through this program. For example, you probably feel somewhat differently about self-stimulation or masturbation than you did before beginning this book. We hope that you're discovering what is right and natural for *you* sexually, and not putting restrictions and expectations on yourself. For instance, you may have found that relaxation exercises, certain fantasies, or reading erotic literature contribute to your ability to get in a sexual mood. And perhaps a lubricant makes touching yourself a more sensitive and pleasurable experience. Try seeing the use of a vibrator as an avenue for exploring what is right and natural for you.

Women often have concerns about experiencing orgasm with the help of a vibrator. They may feel that the orgasm will be an artificial one, something that they can't take credit for or feel good about. Actually, becoming aroused and orgasmic through the use of a vibrator is the same basic (and natural) physical experience as arousal and orgasm through other forms of self-stimulation. Also, remember that there is a person behind the machine! *You* are in control of the vibrator. You will find that, just as you had to explore different kinds of hand strokes and touches that felt best, you will have to experiment with adjusting the pressure and focus of vibrator stimulation in a similar way. Although the vibrator provides a constant source of stimulation, *you* are the one who selects the most pleasurable means of experiencing it.

If you have a partner and are concerned about his feelings about a vibrator, you may want to have him read this chapter and exchange positive and negative feelings with him. We often suggest that the male partner try out the vibrator on his own (see the exercises below) over his whole body. Some men enjoy vibrator stimulation on their genitals; other men feel it's too intense. Either way, almost all couples can find a use for the vibrator that is pleasurable for them. We talk about several ways for couples to use the vibrator in Chapter 9. Right now, you may want to try and explore its nonsexual, sensual, or relaxing pleasures when you are together. Begin by using the vibrator on different muscle areas of each other's body (excluding the genitals)—especially the back, neck, arm, and leg muscles. Try different things and see if you can find some ways that a vibrator adds a little extra enjoyment or relaxation.

It's natural for you to have some reservations before trying something new. However, we think that it is possible for you to see using vibrators as you see using other electrical devices: as a convenience you use some of the time to make life easier, more pleasant, and more interesting.

What exactly is a vibrator? Basically, a vibrator is a relatively small machine—one that you can hold in your hand—that vibrates with a rapid steady thythm. Vibrators are either battery powered or plug into electrical outlets. They come in different shapes and sizes: Some have settings for high and low speeds of vibration, attachments for massaging different body parts, and even (on the more expensive varieties) warmth for massaging sore muscles. Some you hold in your hand (see drawings B and C) and others fit over your hand and cause your fingers and hand to vibrate (Drawing A).

Vibrators are wonderful for massaging your body in order to help you relax and to soothe sore muscles. And they can also provide very pleasurable sensations on your genitals. This isn't surprising when you think about it. When you stimulate your genitals with your finger(s), you rub, stroke, and massage. This is what vibrators do at a faster rate, more steadily, and more intensely than most people can achieve with hand stimulation. Some women need this quality of genital stimulation, especially when they are learning to have orgasms.

Perhaps the biggest concern you may have about trying a vibrator is that you may enjoy it, become orgasmic, and be hooked on using it forever. Being afraid that you may become "addicted" will make it hard for you to relax and be comfortable enough with using a vibrator to allow you to enjoy any pleasurable sensations that the vibrator provides.

Right now, try to relax and give yourself a chance to grow. Most women are able to learn other ways of reaching orgasm once they become orgasmic with the help of a vibrator. At the end of this chapter, we will discuss things that you (or at some point, you and a partner) can do to expand your orgasmic responsiveness after you've had a few orgasms. For now, give yourself a chance to discover if this form of additional stimulation is enjoyable and will work for you.

FINDING THE RIGHT VIBRATOR

Do some shopping around. Vibrators (sometimes they are called massagers) are sold in most department stores, some store catalogues, mail order catalogues, discount houses, and pharmacies. They are very popular because of all of the uses they

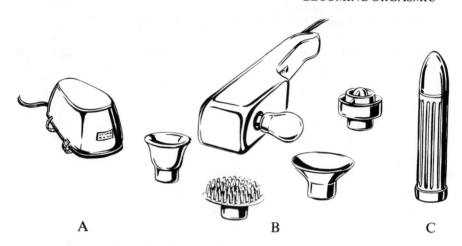

A   B   C

serve—massage, aids to relaxation, and general body stimulation—so there is no real reason to feel embarrassed about purchasing one.

Try to compare a few different models. Do they feel comfortable to hold and do they fit on your hand well? How does the weight feel? Will your arm or hand tire? If you can, have each model you consider plugged in or turned on so you can feel the vibrations. Some models will just feel "better" to you. Make sure you buy a vibrator that is well built, safe, light, and not so big that it is clumsy. We do not recommend battery powered vibrators at this stage (Drawing C), although later on you may want one as an extra. We have found two vibrators that women seem to enjoy particularly. One is an over-the-hand model made by Oster, which is available at most department stores. (Drawing A.) The other is a hand-held model called the Prelude (Drawing B). This vibrator is not as widely available in stores but may be ordered from the Sensory Research Corporation, 5 Lawrence Street, Building 5, Bloomfield, New Jersey, 07003. Variations on these name brands are also available in most major store catalogues, if you prefer to shop for them by mail. If you have a partner, you might want him to shop for a vibrator with you since you will be using the vibrator together at a later point.

USING THE VIBRATOR

Set the stage as you usually do for a self-pleasuring session. Put lotion or oil on your body if you like. *Never use the vibrator around water,* such as when you are in a bath. Begin exploring your body with the vibrator. Explore your face, scalp, neck, shoulders, arms, hands, breasts, and so on, working down your body. After a while move the vibrator over your genitals. You may be surprised at how intense the vibrations feel, particularly around your clitoris. As you did in the earlier steps with the your fingers, try varying pressure, movements, and placement of the vibrator. If it comes with different attachments, try them. If you have a strap-on hand vibrator, try putting one or two fingers in your vagina while you are exploring your genitals. Take your time. Don't try for arousal. Relax and begin to learn how your body responds to this new stimulation. After you have tried this for about 15 minutes, think about the following questions.

1. What differences, if any, did you notice between using the vibrator and using your fingers for stimulation?

2. Were there any areas that were too sensitive to touch directly with the vibrator? Some women find their nipples and clitoris too sensitive for direct stimulation. If this was true for you, the next time try light, barely brushing types of strokes. If your genitals feel particularly sensitive, you might try stimulating yourself to one side of the clitoris, or through some underpants, the first few times. Gradually your body will be able to tolerate more and more direct stimulation. Sometimes women use a small towel over their genitals to diffuse the intensity. If you do this, make sure that the towel does not rub your genitals in a way that absorbs your natural vaginal lubrication. This will cause redness, irritation, and burning.

Do this general body exploration at least two times. When you feel comfortable, concentrate stimulation on your genitals and remember to use fantasy, erotic literature, or the orgasm triggers to enhance your arousal. You can also use your other hand at the same time you are using the vibrator. This way you can provide additional breast or genital stimulation for yourself.

A reasonable amount of time is probably 15 minutes the first three times, then try for 15–30 minutes and then 30–45 minutes, if that's what your body needs. It is not unusual for 30–45 minutes of intense genital stimulation to be necessary when you're learning to become orgasmic. Again, don't worry about how long it's taking you. Your body is capable of orgasm; it just needs to be encouraged. Stay at this step at least two weeks or six individual self-pleasuring sessions that last at least 30–40 minutes. Remember to use what you've learned in earlier chapters—fantasy, erotic literature, orgasm triggers or whatever else works for you—in order to increase your sensual pleasure with the vibrator.

AFTER A FEW WEEKS

If you haven't had orgasm up to this point, you may feel very discouraged. If you find this happening, you may want to continue a while longer with manual and vibrator self-stimulation, particularly if you feel you may be getting close to orgasm. Or, if you have a partner, you may want to move ahead to Chapter 8—some women make additional progress with their partner. Whatever you decide to do, take a moment to think about what you *have* learned, and in what ways you have grown sexually. There really is no such thing as an unimportant change. Try to give yourself credit for making the gains you have made; that's a sign that with time, more changes are going to happen.

Perhaps you've had an orgasm. It's not uncommon for women to be somewhat surprised by the experience. Your ideas and expectations about what orgasm would be like may or may not have been true for you. Perhaps you expected much more:

> All of a sudden the sensations just stopped and I couldn't go on . . . it was too sensitive there. It was nice but not much to celebrate.

> It seemed as if I was rubbing my clitoris for about 20 minutes then the feelings just sort of changed all of a sudden. I think it was an orgasm but I wasn't sure.

Or perhaps you expected much less:

> I was feeling pretty turned on and this time instead of staying at that level or stopping, I kept on using the vibrator and my hand too. Suddenly I had this warm pulsating *strong* feeling come over me. It was terrific! I tried to do it again right away but with no luck.

Also, it's not unusual for women to have mixed feelings about becoming orgasmic—happiness or relief, along with some feelings of disappointment. This is natural; and perhaps you've felt this way about other events in your life—such as a vacation you've planned, getting a new job, or doing anything you've looked forward to for a long time. Hopefully, you feel good about yourself! You've overcome some obstacles and experienced a pleasure that is truly yours alone. Women sometimes feel more secure about themselves. Some women have excitedly called us right after their first orgasm. Other women are pleased, but discover that orgasm really is only part of their greater sexual satisfaction. Whatever you feel, orgasm has helped you to know yourself better—and whether or not you share this knowledge with a partner, it's part of you now. You can be proud of all the changes you have experienced and assure yourself that there's more growth ahead.

IF YOU LIKED THE VIBRATOR, BUT . . .

Whether or not you've had an orgasm yet, hopefully you feel good about what you've experienced with the vibrator. Yet, as we mentioned earlier, you may be concerned that you are or will become too dependent on it. Most women we have seen become orgasmic and enjoy the vibrator a lot, but gradually they are able to get an equal amount of satisfaction from other kinds of stimulation. Here are some suggestions to broaden your orgasmic responsiveness.

If you have experienced orgasm with a vibrator, or feel that with a little more time, it might happen, let yourself get used to these new sexual response patterns. Let yourself have several sessions with orgasm. Then, if you are interested in expanding your arousal to manual stimulation, gradually include more and more hand stimulation into your sessions. Expect to spend more time (vibrator arousal usually occurs more quickly) bringing yourself to high levels of arousal manually. Sometimes stronger orgasms come after longer periods of sexual arousal.

You can incorporate manual stimulation in a variety of ways. For instance, you might try letting yourself get quite highly sexually aroused with your vibrator and then putting it aside and continuing with your hands. Doing this may mean that your arousal level does not continue to increase as rapidly; it may even drop some. If your arousal drops, you may be tempted to give up in discouragement. Try not to let this happen—it's natural for things to slow down when you first switch types of stimulation. And remember, you have plenty of time. Continue to give yourself manual stimulation for as long as it's pleasurable.

The next time you try switching from the vibrator to manual stimulation, you might try reaching a very high level of arousal and then changing to manual stimulation during the last few seconds before orgasm, or just as your orgasm begins, so that during orgasm you are using your hands without a vibrator. Once you have an orgasm in this way, you can try changing the point at which you concentrate on hand stimulation, gradually moving that point closer and closer to the beginning of your self-stimulation session.

Another possibility that may help you expand your ability to become aroused is to simultaneously use both your hand and the vibrator throughout your sessions. This can be very erotic, since you are providing yourself with quite a variety of sensations—different textures, tempos, and pressures. Over your sessions you can gradually begin to spend more time focusing on manual stimulation and less time focusing on vibrator stimulation. It's important to just try this for short periods in the beginning. For instance: Let yourself get a little aroused using both hand and vibrator, then for a few seconds just try using your hand (or both hands); go back to hand and vibrator for a minute or two; then continue without the vibrator for a few seconds longer, and so on. Slowly (over several sessions) increase the amount of time you use your hands without the vibrator. Eventually (and this may mean several weeks) you may be able to have some of your sessions with little if any use of the vibrator. During your sessions, try not to be concerned about how aroused you are.

Concentrate on your physical sensations and the pleasure they are giving you.

Suppose, however, that you find, even with repeated experimentation, that you *prefer* vibrator stimulation. A number of women do find that even though they might be able to be orgasmic through manual masturbation, the intense, regular stimulation that a vibrator provides is more pleasurable. If you enjoy the vibrator and always want to use it to enhance your sexual responsiveness, that's great! You do not *have* to be able to masturbate without a vibrator, particularly if you find, as many women do, that it's a good source of sexual pleasure. Let yourself grow with it! Decide what you would like *for yourself*.

WHERE TO GO FROM HERE

You are now at a very special place in your sexual growth. If you look back to your first exercise in Chapter 2, you will see that you've made quite a lot of progress. We'd like you to take a few minutes and think about some of the changes you've made and how you feel about yourself at this point. You might want to look back at some of the goals for this program we discussed in Chapter 1.

We hope that after progressing through Chapters 1–7, you feel more comfortable with your body and have a better understanding of how feelings about yourself as a person relate to your sexuality. We hope that you are more aware of the broad range of what is "normal" sexual functioning. You are becoming more in touch with physical sensations and with sexual thoughts and feelings. Also, you have a better idea of what does or does not help you feel relaxed, of what puts you in an emotionally receptive mood for sex, and you know some ways to focus and concentrate on your body in order to enhance the quality of your sexual feelings.

Along the way you have probably confronted a few of your fears and inhibitions. Because of this, you are better able to enjoy your body for the pleasure it can give you, and you feel more open to exploring and expanding new areas of your sexuality.

Whether you've made all or some of these changes, and whether or not you've achieved orgasm yet, you've already come a long way.

The next three chapters deal with ways to enhance your sexual experiences with a partner. It is written for the woman who has never been, or is infrequently, orgasmic with a partner. It is not necessary for you to have had an orgasm for you to go on to this next section. If you feel satisfied with the progress you've made and find that you are able to bring yourself to fairly high levels of arousal in your individual sessions, you may want to move on. On the other hand, you may feel you need to spend more time on your own before beginning new experiences with your partner. Spend some time thinking and perhaps talking with your partner about what you feel would be best for you.

If you do not currently have a partner but expect to have one at some later time in your life, you may want to read this section also.

8

Sharing Self Discoveries with Your Partner

Up to this point, your partner has only been able to share indirectly in your newfound feelings and discoveries. He may be somewhat of a stranger to the things you have been practicing for these past sessions. The next few exercises will give you a chance to share your discoveries with your partner. Right now we would like him to read this section along with you.

Before we talk about this step, we would like to note where you might be in your sexual growth right now. You may not have experienced your first orgasm yet—that's okay. What is most important is that you have learned how to give yourself a fairly high level of sexually arousing pleasure. Continue to use your individual masturbation sessions to teach yourself about what feels good and keep your sexual arousal high. Some women experience their first orgasm *with* their partner, and this might happen for you.

This step is a challenging one in some ways. You will gradually be teaching your partner about what kinds of stimulation give you pleasure. At first you may want to just discuss what works for you—the kinds of stimulation you need—like vibrators, manual stimulation, certain strokes and pressures—and then you will try a self-pleasuring session with your partner next to you. Your partner can also share with you his patterns of masturbation. This is a unique opportunity for you both to learn how each of you gives your own body pleasure so that you can learn more about pleasuring each other.

How do you feel about masturbating in front of your partner? Often, when women begin to try to get aroused with their partner present, they find it a bit difficult. This difficulty may be partly a result of feeling distracted—someone else is in the room with you. It also may be somewhat embarrassing, since most of us have grown up with a taboo against doing anything sexual in front of another person. Or you may be worried about what your partner will think—whether or not he will like this new aspect of you—especially if many of your past sexual experiences together have been unpleasant. We will talk about this again in a moment.

For now, whatever your feelings are, and you probably have some that we haven't mentioned, feel confident that it is completely natural to have mixed emotions about sharing your progress with a partner. The most important aspect of your future sexual experiences together is that you give each other encouragement and support—both physically and emotionally. Support that is meaningful for you both includes all sorts of things, but basically support means providing feelings of understanding and encouragement without pressure or criticism. We will make some specific suggestions in a moment which will make it easier for you both to create a good atmosphere in which to try this exercise.

Before you decide whether or not you want to try this exercise, we would like you and your partner to talk over any expectations or apprehensions that you may have. You can do this in many different ways. We would like to make the following suggestions: Imagine that you are going to begin pleasuring yourself in front of each other. What concerns do you think *you* would have? What concerns do you think *your partner* would have? Whether or not you "guess right" about your partner is less important than just exchanging your concerns about each other's feelings. Talk about each feeling in terms of what each of you can do to maximize the pleasure and minimize the mutual worries. Share what your fears and hopes are for this experience.

Exploring the above should give you a clearer idea of how each of you feels about doing this exercise, whatever those feelings might be. It should also give you an idea of what you are each hoping to gain from this experience.

You might also consider how you *both* see masturbation fitting or not fitting into your total sexual relationship. Do you see it only as something to be done in "emergencies"—when one partner is away or sick? Spend a few minute discussing this, because we will come back to it again later.

If you do decide that masturbation really has very little or no place in your sexual relationship, you may find the idea of sharing this activity very unacceptable. You do not have to believe that masturbation is enjoyable or valuable to your sexual relationship in order to do this exercise. The primary purpose here is simple: to show your partner what you've learned about yourself. Only you really know how to give yourself the kind of stimulation you need to become sexually aroused. You are your partner's best teacher of what gives you pleasure. Although it may be difficult at first, we have seen couples grow sexually and emotionally from trying this experience.

In speaking with other couples in therapy, we noticed that their concerns and reservations often centered around several frequent themes. We'd like to suggest these for you to talk about if you haven't already, especially if you found it somewhat difficult to express and exchange your feelings with each other.

From the woman's point of view, for instance, what does it mean to you to touch yourself or give yourself pleasure with your partner watching you? Are you pleased, frightened, uncertain, or are you just curious? We expect your feelings to be a mixture of interest and hesitation: interest because this is something new that you have never shared before; and hesitation because you don't really know how difficult or easy it will be with him present, and perhaps also because you do not know how he will respond to you in this new situation. If you feel your partner will be somehow critical, discuss this with him. What *exactly* are you afraid that he might think or say?

As we mentioned earlier, trying this step may conflict with some of the sexual values that you learned while growing up. Masturbation, in most homes, is not regarded as an acceptable form of sexual expression. It is usually done in private, if not on the sly. Therefore, masturbating with someone else present may feel a bit like being "caught in the act." Several things can be done to reduce these feelings. One is sharing and supporting each other's attempts in the positive ways you have discussed above. Another is just to try—repeated attempts will help you re-evaluate some of the old values you have gathered throughout your development.

Another sexual value that may contribute to some uneasiness is the expectation that married couples (or more generally, any couple in a relationship) are not supposed to masturbate. Masturbation is thought to be detrimental or unnecessary if a partner is available. This view sees masturbation as a distant second- or third-rate sexual activity, in comparison to intercourse and other mutual kinds of stimulation. Often, masturbation is thought to be detrimental because of the erroneous belief that sexual desire or energy will be used up and result in a loss of desire for couple sex. Actually, this is not true. In fact, research on female sexuality has found that women who masturbate are more likely to be orgasmic and to engage in sexual expression of all forms. A large number of men and women *do* masturbate after marriage. It's possible to see masturbation as another sexual avenue to explore and grow from, particularly since you will be sharing positive changes with your partner.

And from the man's point of view, which aspects of this step are you looking forward to enjoying, and which do you think will be more difficult? Even the most enthusiastic male partners often have some reservations before doing this exercise. Usually reservations revolve around the following concerns: a) The man feels left out, unimportant and uninvolved in the woman's self-pleasuring; b) and, as a result, he has a nagging doubt that he is somehow replaceable—that his partner will prefer her own stimulation to his.

With almost all the couples that we have seen in therapy, the woman does learn to enjoy self-pleasuring but wants primarily to have sex with her partner. What she learns about her body during her own sessions will make it easier for her to teach you the most pleasurable ways to stimulate her. And, as we mentioned above, masturbation does not interfere with the desire for mutual sex. In fact, for many women, it seems to enhance sexual desire. It offers a different kind of emotional satisfaction. So even though you may develop a very satisfying mutual sexual relationship, you can still enjoy masturbation.

There are ways in which you can increase your involvement with your partner. A very important aspect of the next few sexual sessions you do together is for you to let her show you or tell you what gives her pleasure. That may sound easy, but our experience has shown us that this is a difficult thing to put into practice. Men in our culture are *expected* to know what to do sexually with their partners at all times, and not knowing somehow reflects on their competence as a man and as a lover. Of course, this is unreasonable—the same sexual technique will not be equally pleasurable to all women, and we have tried to stress that the same woman also varies in her preferences at different times. Nevertheless, you may occasionally have to remind yourself that a good lover is one who tries to pleasure his partner in a way that is specifically good for her. This involves real intimacy and communication and forms the foundation from which you can eventually expand your sexuality as a couple.

Men are influenced by the same cultural values about masturbation as are women. Years of believing that one should not be caught in the act, or that it is not right to combine masturbation and a close relationship with someone else, are not going to disappear automatically. Also, the cultural expectation that men are supposed to be super sexual is an added burden on men. This expectation suggests that any sexual experience, including sharing masturbation, should be easy for men. Actually, many men do not find it easy to masturbate in front of their partner. If this is true for you, try and express your concerns about this to your partner. In any case, the woman's encouragement and support—in whatever ways are best for you—is very important. Let her know what she can do to make this experience a positive one for you both.

Perhaps one or both of you feel strongly that you do not want to do this sharing exercise. Or perhaps you attempt it but feel extremely uncomfortable or upset afterwards. That's okay; it does not mean there is something wrong with you. Rather, it means that this particular learning experience is not suited to your needs. Finish reading this chapter, since other information is included, and then go on to Chapter 9. In other words, *this exercise is optional, one that you both should feel similarly comfortable about trying.* If you don't, just read through Chapter 8 (particularly the section on "Initiation and Refusal") and move ahead to Chapter 9, which will provide you with other ways to learn to pleasure each other.

SPECIFIC SUGGESTIONS FOR SELF-PLEASURING WITH YOUR PARTNER

It is not unusual to feel awkward or somewhat uncomfortable touching yourself in front of your mate. You shouldn't feel that you are "performing" but rather that you are teaching. Talking

about ways to decrease your discomfort is a first step. There are
also several things you can do to enhance your session. The first
time that you try these suggestions, it may feel a bit strange for
both of you; obviously, we don't expect you to have no difficulty
the first time. This, after all, is still a period of mutual discovery—
not a demonstration of expertise.

Your partner is not expected to arouse you sexually; he (or
she) is expected to make it as easy as possible for you to arouse
yourself. The following are some specific suggestions that have
helped a variety of other couples who followed this program.
We hope that you will find some that feel right for you, or that
you will make up your own.

1. Both of you help set the mood for this session. You may want
soft light or candlelight in the room to make the atmosphere seem
warmer and more private. You need enough light so that you can
see each other, but not so much that you will feel uncomfortable.

Some couples like to have a glass of wine together before they begin, or just sit and talk a while. This is not a good time to solve daily problems or crises, however. So try to talk about pleasant topics or discuss any feelings of anticipation you may have about what you are about to try.

2. Both of you should be nude. A shower together is one way to get nude comfortably. Sharing warm water and soapsuds helps put people in a relaxed and sensual mood. Or, if you don't want to shower, you might want to undress each other slowly and kiss or caress each other as you do. (Remember to make sure that the room is a comfortable temperature to be in without clothes.)

If you are not used to being nude in front of your partner, you might wear a loose-fitting shirt or nightgown. It should be something that you feel good about wearing and something that will still allow your partner to see your particular techniques of masturbating easily. You may find that you gradually become more comfortable during your session together and eventually you should try to be completely undressed. But if this is a bit scary, go slowly. Once again, practice and partner support will help you feel more at ease.

3. Begin with some mutual exchange of pleasure—hugging, kissing, light stroking of each other's face or body, and whatever else you like. Concentrate on feeling good and on the physical sensations that your body is providing. When the women is ready, she can begin to show her partner the ways in which she touches herself which give her pleasure. Later in the session, or during the next session, the man may want to stimulate himself so that she can learn from him.

People differ in their needs for partner support during their own masturbation—for example, you may want your partner touching you, holding you, or just lying next to you as you are masturbating. Do whatever would make you feel most comfortable, while also asking what your partner prefers. This helps both partners to feel involved.

4. You may want to try this exercise again, so don't worry if you can't see every detail of what your partner is doing. What you should pay attention to at first is your partner's movements, the various areas of his/her body that he/she caresses, and the kind of touches that are used.

5. End the session with some mutual affection and then talk to each other about how you felt during this exercise. Also ask questions about things you were not sure about. For instance, "What kind of stroke were you using on your clitoris?" "Did your fingers go inside your vagina, too? How far?" "How hard were you pressing on your breasts? Clitoris?" and "How much time did you spend touching your scrotum?" "How strong was your grip on your penis?" If you decide to repeat this exercise, use what you learned from the first session in order to improve the experience. Each time you do self-pleasuring with each other, notice what your partner repeats during each session, and also notice what she or he does differently. It is important for you to realize that you both have different needs and responses, and that you will not respond exactly the same way during each sexual experience.

POTENTIAL DIFFICULTIES

Women sometimes find it difficult to experience feelings of pleasure during this exercise. They are either distracted by their partner's presence, or worried about his reaction to their sexual responses. If this happens to you, there are several ways you might deal with it. You might have him move into a position that is more supportive and less distracting, perhaps with him sitting behind you and holding you (see Chapter 9). Alternatively, you may find his touch distracting at this time; you may like him just to be near you. Another technique to help you not be distracted is to close your eyes and create a fantasy—you might even imagine that you are alone rather than with your partner.

Remember that trying for arousal will only make things more difficult for you. It is not necessary for you to have an orgasm during these sessions. Instead, try to feel comfortable showing your partner what you like, and then gradually let yourself become more expressive in his presence. It may take a while, so give yourself time. *Whatever* you are able to do is a sign of change to build upon. Enjoy yourself for what you can do and don't fall into the trap of judging (or letting your partner judge) your progress by where you think you ought to be.

Some women, on the other hand, have no difficulty feeling pleasure or even becoming aroused during their first sharing experience with their partner. If you did become aroused or experienced orgasm, were you surprised? Pleased? You should be! Did you like the way that your partner responded to your self-pleasuring? If so, let him know. Particularly let him know the ways in which he helped you feel at ease enough to be sexually expressive with him beside you. If he didn't respond in a way that made you feel good, think about what you can tell him to do or say that would make a difference to you.

The man who has had his first experience seeing his partner become aroused or have an orgasm may not know quite how to respond, or what to feel. It's not uncommon for men to feel somewhat awkward or left out, even if you talked this over earlier and didn't expect him to react this way. Another possible reaction for the male partner is some apprehension about seeing his partner being sexually responsive, especially if this is a first. What does it mean for her to be sexual and enjoy it?

Some men are concerned that a sexually responsive woman will want sex all the time. The thought of a "super" sexual partner can scare a man since most men have some concerns about their own performance; or he may worry that she will seek sex with a lot of different partners in addition to himself. Worries about out-of-control sexual urges can be a concern for women also—they sometimes think that after a few orgasms they will want sex all the time and never be satisfied. In point of fact, based on the couples we have seen in sex therapy, the frequency of sex and the choice of sexual partners is not really related to whether the woman is orgasmic or not. What does change is the amount of pleasure both partners derive from each sexual encounter. Their increased satisfaction seems only partly related to the fact that the woman is able to have orgasms, and more related to greater comfort and to the ability to mutually communicate sexual needs.

WHAT YOU CAN GAIN

There are several new doors that we hope will be opened by trying this step. Sharing pleasure is a very intimate experience; and sharing personal sexual pleasure means that trust and understanding are an important part of a couple's feelings for each other. We hope that with increased openness about sharing the pleasure you've found, your mutual feelings of trust deepen. In addition, rather than necessarily just being a transitory "step," we hope that this experience broadens the range of sexual activities that you can do and that you desire to do with one another. You may find this a very pleasurable experience that you will want to include among the things you do together. And finally, we hope your ability to try this builds a sense of *personal* satisfaction for you both.

INITIATION AND REFUSAL

A common area that many couples want to improve upon is their pattern of suggesting (initiating) and refusing sexual activities. Although you may not find this to be a problem at the moment, you probably have had experiences in which feeling more comfortable and confident about initiating and refusing would benefit you both.

Think for a minute about how your partner usually initiates sex. With a kiss? A touch? A look? A grab? A few words? Initiating and refusing sexual advances are very important aspects of sexual communication, ones that cause difficulty for almost everyone. Generally, the problem seems to be: How do you manage to get two people in the *mood* at the same *time* and at a time when sex is possible?

It's natural for two people to have differences as to when and how often sex is desired. For women, desire for sex can increase and decrease at times during the menstrual cycle. For instance, some women report increased arousal during the middle of their cycle and right before menstrual flow. However, these changes in sexual desire do not seem to be very consistent and some women do not notice any fluctuations in desire that are related to their cycle. The same statement is true for birth control pills with some women reporting greater desire and others reporting less desire after being on the pill for a while.

Other influences on sexual desire include illness, pregnancy, depression and aging. You've probably noticed that when you are ill, uncomfortable, or upset your interest in sex decreases. This may or may not occur during pregnancy and aging, since some people feel very good at these times and others feel physically or emotionally distressed. Also, although there is no physiological reason to avoid sex during a woman's menstrual flow, some women have pain or discomfort at this time; other women do not experience discomfort and actually enjoy the closeness of sex at this time.

With variations in sexual desire, for whatever reasons, there are times when one partner initiates and the other refuses. But there may be other influences affecting whether on person initiates and the other says "yes" or "no." What we would like you to do is to "brainstorm" on what the problems are for you two on the issue of initiating and refusing sex. In brainstorming, the idea is to mention many different things without criticizing them. Just let your ideas flow. Think about who usually initiates. Would you like the other person to do more? Who usually refuses, and how does this make you both feel? Talk about what makes it difficult to get sex started: for instance, the presence of children, feeling tired at the end of the day, or having household chores to do first.

Certainly a very basic consideration is timing. One woman who was in therapy complained that her husband always began "fooling around" with her while she was doing dishes or scrubbing the bathtub—not exactly a time when she felt very sexy!

More frequently, couples tend to put sex off until the very end of their day—when they are tired. If this describes your situation, you may want to think about any adjustments you could make in your schedules to spend time together earlier. The question is one of priorities: If sex is important to both of you, then it shouldn't be last on your list after all other activities. This will probably mean that you have to help each other free up some time. The man, for instance, might share some of the housework and help take care of the children's needs if that has been primarily the woman's responsibility and usually keeps her busy in the evenings. The woman may, on the other hand, help guarantee some uninterrupted time for her partner so that he can finish up any of his responsibilities, and vice versa.

Sometimes one partner initiates in a way that does not appeal to the other partner. Blowing in his ear or nibbling on her neck may do nothing to encourage, and may even discourage his or her interest. We have found a very useful exercise you can do together that will help you both learn good ways to initiate sex ("good" in terms of what your partner likes). We would like you to do an exercise we call *Reverse Role-Play*: To do this, pretend you are your partner and that your partner is you, and act out what you consider to be a *poor* initiation. For instance, the woman takes the role of the man and demonstrates what a poor initiation by him is like. Set the typical scene (such as in the living room or the bedroom) as well as the action (a grab for the breast, a quick kiss). Then tell your partner what you would prefer and why. Be specific. Physically and verbally demonstrate to the other person how they could initiate sex that would make you feel good. Now have your partner practice different *good* initiations a few times with your help. Take turns so that you both get a chance to demonstrate what kinds of initiations are good and bad for you, and why.

But even the best initiation will not always be accepted. Have you ever had the feeling that you couldn't tell your partner "no," or have you ever felt resentful about accepting? It is possible to say no in a way that's not hurtful for the other person. Indicating that your care about your partner, or that you'd like to be with him or her but don't feel like sex, or discussing why you aren't in the mood now but would like to after you finish your work or tomorrow morning, are some possibilities. A blunt "no" or "I'm tired" is likely to make the other person feel hurt and rejected, and it can be a good basis for a fight.

So, as you did before, pretend you are your partner and role-play a *bad refusal*—some way that makes you feel angry or resentful when you initiate and are refused. Again set the scene and act out the words or gestures your partner uses. Then point out what would make it a good refusal and act that out. Let your partner try it too. Practice so that you understand what your partner means by a *good* refusal. Have your partner practice accepting the refusal as well. Saying something which shows that you acknowledge and accept the fact that your partner cannot have or doesn't want sex right now helps relieve feelings of tension and guilt.

There are two other areas that contribute to good initiation or refusal communication. We have found that often couples benefit from discussing the following topics: How frequently would each of you like to have sex? Here, you should be clear on whether sex always includes intercourse. There may be times when non-sexual affection, sensual pleasuring with a vibrator, manual or oral stimulation to orgasm would be preferred by your partner.

Often one partner wants sex more frequently than the other. If this is the case, one partner is going to be initiating a lot, while the other partner is refusing a lot. It sometimes helps to decide on a reasonable compromise of about how often to have sex so that initiations are less frequent and thus are more likely to be accepted.

Another area that couples often find to be a problem is the pattern of one person doing most of the initiating. There are various reasons why this causes difficulty: 1) It can leave one partner feeling less desired than the other if he or she is always taking the first step; 2) it tends to make sexual activities more dependent on just one person's mood and needs; 3) it sets up roles where one person's responsibility is almost always to decide when to have sex while the other person always holds the stamp of acceptance or refusal; and 4) sometimes, because the pattern is so predictable and the roles are set, it can contribute to making your sex life boring. However, many couples do have preferred pattern in which one person does almost all of the initiating. If this is your pattern and you *both* like it, there is no reason to change as long as the other person feels free to initiate if they find they want to.

If, however, you would like to initiate more or have your partner initiate more, you can work on making this possible. First, try talking about why you would like yourself or your partner to initiate more. Some couples just like the idea of equalizing their sexual initiations—it makes sex seem more mutual and can make one partner feel less "used" at the whim of the other. Whatever your reasons are, talk them over together.

Secondly, the person who is to increase their initiating probably has some concerns about doing so. One concern is how your partner will respond—what if your partner turns down your initiation? Talk about your reservations and what you can do to maximize, at least at first, your chances of not being refused (the better time, place, mood). Keep in mind what we discussed earlier about refusals not being a rejection of you as a person.

And thirdly, for women who are learning to initiate more, there are some special difficulties. In our culture, women are taught that the male should usually initiate more often and even though they would personally like to change their own pattern, they feel conflicted about it. Discuss this with your partner. Give him a chance to tell you why he would like it and reassure you about any fears you have such as feeling too aggressive or "unfeminine." Usually men welcome the chance to have their partner initiate more. A major motivation for many women to be more assertive sexually is simply the freedom to be able to express themselves—to be able to say what they would like to do. You will be doing more of this in your sexual activities as a couple as you continue through the next few chapters.

9

Pleasuring Each Other

Pleasuring each other is a process of exploration and growth similar to the stages you went through in getting in touch with your own body. The first step is becoming comfortable enough to explore new possibilities for pleasure that your body and your partner's touch can give you. In order to feel really free to do this, you both need to first consider your expectations for your sessions together.

EXPECTATIONS

Do you have any expectations about how your sessions together will be in comparison with your individual sessions? It's natural for you to think about this. If you were able to become highly aroused or orgasmic through individual self-stimulation, you may be expecting the same thing to happen automatically in your couple sessions. Or perhaps you are expecting your couple sessions not to live up to your individual sessions. Perhaps you were not able to reach orgasm through self-stimulation. You may be thinking that arousal and orgasm will be easier with your partner present. Whatever your expectations are, they are likely to affect what happens between the two of you. You may find yourself overly concerned with tracking your own or your partner's level of arousal and lose touch with any feelings of pleasure within yourself. You may begin putting pressure on yourself or your partner to perform or respond in certain ways, and old feelings of frustration and self-doubt may reappear.

What are some positive expectations for your sessions together? You can expect the process of learning new ways to pleasure each other to take time and understanding. Exploration, discovery, guiding, learning, trusting, and communicating are all necessary for sexual growth. With time and understanding, you are likely to enrich and deepen the intimacy between the two of you. You will probably see gains in other areas of your relationship with growth in your sexual relationship.

You can now take more responsibility for when sessions occur and for what happens during a session. You each need to participate actively in the process of changing together as a couple. Feeling free to initiate (suggest) and refuse a sexual encounter makes for a more mutual physical and emotional relationship.

During a session, you will find yourself giving as well as receiving pleasure. Keep in mind that how you respond sexually can change from sexual encounter to sexual encounter as well as at any given time within a particular session. What feels good at one time may be neutral or even unpleasant at another time. For example, some women find breast stimulation painful or neutral (not particularly pleasant or unpleasant) early in a session, but extremely enjoyable after they become somewhat aroused. Also, some men find having their nipples touched or kissed pleasurable once aroused, whereas this may feel "ticklish" at other times. Some women want to avoid breast caressing completely before or during the early part of their menstrual period because their breasts are tender. These normal variations in personal preferences make communication extremely important.

VERBAL AND NONVERBAL COMMUNICATION

There are many different ways people can communicate. Infants can make themselves understood with a few grunts or cries. We all encounter daily situations in which the look in a person's eyes or their facial expression communicates feelings such as pleasure, disapproval, delight, or anger. In the next few sessions, you will be focusing on using verbal and nonverbal communication to help guide your partner in pleasuring you. For example, if the woman's breasts are being kissed or touched, she might say, "That feels good" or perhaps, "Stroking the nipple hurts; try stroking around the nipple." However, rather than speak, the woman might try placing her hand over her partner's hand and guiding it so that he is touching her in the way that feels most pleasant. Both verbal and nonverbal forms of communication are important. As you practice stimulating each other, you should try using both means of communicating.

Learning to communicate so that you both learn from each other and can respond to each other's desires insures, as we mentioned, that each sexual experience is unique and spontaneous. If you can learn to tell each other what you want during sex, you are less likely to fall into a routine, where what you do is the same each time. Getting into a rut sexually usually takes away from feelings of excited anticipation which add so much to the experience.

Perhaps you have done some of this communication of likes and dislikes before, or you may have kept silent during sex because you were afraid that you might hurt your partner's feelings. There is a lot of pressure on men and women these days (particularly on men) to be experts at sex; many believe that if they are "good lovers," they will know (without being told) the right thing to do to please their partner. This kind of situation only increases worries and tensions which interfere with really enjoying yourself sexually. You may feel you have to be a mind reader and be constantly looking for signs and clues at to what your partner wants or is feeling (the spectator role again). You may feel responsible for your partner's sexuality and see his/her sexual responsiveness, and whether or not he/she has an orgasm, as a reflection on you.

Actually you cannot *give* your partner an orgasm. Giving and receiving pleasure means the physical and emotional involvement of *you both*. As a couple, you must share the responsibility for making your sexual encounters as rewarding as possible. You can provide feelings of pleasure and arousal in an environment of comfort, warmth, and caring which will allow your partner to feel like going on to experience orgasm. Sharing involves communicating and trusting; trusting each other to communicate verbally or nonverbally what it is you feel and what it is you would like to do. Trust allows you both to feel free to really get into and to focus on your own pleasure.

It would be natural to feel somewhat uneasy when you first communicate directly about things that have to do with sex. Most of us were not given much chance to practice sexual communication while growing up. Recognizing this will make it easier for you to offer each other support. Saying things such as, "I know you feel embarrassed, I do too," or "That was hard for me to say," gives your partner encouragement and support because it aids understanding and caring. Communicating positively, such as "If you would touch me this way that would feel really good," rather than negatively, "I don't like that" is important. A positive statement shows that you want your partner to try and indirectly says you think he or she *can* learn how to pleasure you. Also, the particular example here gives your partner something specific to try—your message has important information that only you can provide. Communicating your needs is a vital ingredient for the continued renewal and expansion of your sexuality. It keeps sex interesting and alive.

Again, it may be hard for you both not to compare these early couple sessions with your individual sessions. If you were highly aroused or orgasmic during your self-pleasuring sessions, you may be watching yourself for signs of arousal. It's natural for you to feel disappointed if you don't get aroused or as aroused as you do in your individual sessions. This doesn't mean that something is wrong. Give yourself and your partner time to learn to get in touch sexually, just as you gave yourself time.

Some women who have not reached orgasm up to this step do experience orgasm through manual or vibrator stimulation with their partner present. If you weren't orgasmic through the self-stimulation sessions, you may begin to put pressure on yourself and your partner and feelings of frustration and self-doubt may result. You may feel your partner is judging you and watching for any signs of arousal. One thing that will help is for you to continue your individual self-stimulation sessions at other times during the week, so that you are continuing to grow sexually as an individual as well as a couple. Taking the pressure off yourself and your partner—letting yourselves relax and enjoy your sessions together—makes it more likely that you will experience orgasm either through your own or your partner's stimulation during the next few weeks. Talking with your partner about some of the concerns you each have prior to your sessions is also an important way to deal with those reservations.

YOUR SESSIONS: HOW TO BEGIN

Lying close, kissing, massaging, and running your hands along each other's bodies will help set the mood. When you both feel comfortable, one of you begin exploring the other's body with your hands and mouth. Try some tentative touching and kissing of the breasts or chest, ears, back of the neck, inner thighs—any part of the body which gives pleasure. The partner being pleasured should be giving gentle positive communication about what he or she likes. What is said, and the tone of your voice, should indicate whether you like what is being done, and if not, what the person doing the pleasuring should try. Your whole body is involved in sexual response, so take your time and communicate about what does or doesn't feel good.

The process of exploring and communicating can be done one at a time or mutually, as long as each of you has a chance to get into what you're feeling and help guide your partner in stimulating you. Sometimes, you may want to really get involved in just pleasuring your partner or in being pleasured. At other times, you will want to pleasure each other at the same time. Let your partner know.

Gradually include the genitals in your explorations. At first it is probably better for you to take turns giving and receiving pleasure. When you are touching or stimulating your partner's genitals, either manually or with a vibrator, try to recreate the movements, pressures, and pace which your partner likes when stimulating him/her self. The first few times you do this you will probably find you need lots of guidance, but it's the best way to learn. Have the partner who is being pleasured verbally or nonverbally communicate to you what feels best. A nonverbal communication, again, might be placing your hand over your partner's hand and moving or pressing down in order to indicate the kind of stroke you like.

POSITIONS

You may want to (1) lie on your sides facing each other as you do this; (2) lie head to feet so that you each can see each other's genitals; (3) take turns with the pleasurer sitting down next to his/her partner's genitals; or (4) have your partner lie down or sit with his/her back supported against a wall or pillow. The partner who is doing the pleasuring sits between the other's legs so that he/she can easily see and touch his/her partner's genitals, while the person receiving stimulation can totally focus on their own pleasure. (5) For pleasuring the female, the male can sit with his back propped up or leaning against the wall. The woman then sits between his legs facing away from him. Her back is against his chest. In this position the male can encircle the woman with his arms and touch her breasts and genitals, as well as kiss her neck and hair. The woman can lean back against her partner for support and is free to concentrate on her own pleasure. It is important to become familiar with the different parts of each other's bodies. Take your time—the idea is not to arouse each other. As a matter of fact, it would probably interfere with sharing for you to try for arousal at this point.

Try and have at least three to six sessions where you focus on teaching and learning the most effective ways of communicating and giving pleasure. Seeing where you are touching is a good idea the first few times you do this. If after two sessions you feel comfortable with stimulating each other, have a session where you both use what you've learned. During this session, do whatever things you like to pleasure each other except intercourse. You should probably allow 30 minutes to one hour for each couple session. If orgasm happens, that's fine, but do not expect it or try for it at first. The important thing is to make each session as pleasurable and rewarding as possible. Orgasm does not have to be the goal or end point of your sessions. Hopefully, you will experience some good feelings in your body, be able to help your partner achieve good feelings in his/her body, and feel closer as a couple. Orgasm will come in time if you continue to be attuned to your feelings of sexual pleasure, and to share those feelings in an atmosphere of warmth and concern.

THINGS TO THINK ABOUT
AND TALK OVER WITH EACH OTHER

1. What do you feel you still need to work on?
2. Where do you see progress being made?
3. If you have not reached orgasm yet, how do you or your partner feel about this?

After having several couple sessions you may find you are thinking about or feeling concerned about certain things. We'd like to help you begin to explore some of these thoughts and feelings.

How do you feel about sex without intercourse? Perhaps you feel some satisfaction with whatever gains you've made up this point. You may be eager to go on to intercourse, and see pleasuring through other means as a poor substitute. Such feelings may be causing you to rush through your sessions, and they probably make it hard for you to relax and enjoy yourself and to flow with what your body is experiencing. You may feel better if you keep in mind that the things you are learning will make intercourse a more enjoyable experience. These "foreplay" or pleasuring techniques can be a prelude to intercourse or ends in themselves. We will talk more about this in the next chapter on intercourse.

If you engaged in petting and genital touching before marriage and felt guilty about it, it would be natural for you to have some of those same reservations now, even though you're older, married, or in a stable relationship. You may still associate genital touching with shame, guilt, or anxiety even though circumstances have changed.

Talking about these feelings with a supportive partner may help. It is possible to change your attitudes and ideas about what you do sexually, especially if you see some advantage in this. One advantage is that broadening the range or variety of sexual activities you and your partner enjoy can only add to the spontaneity and genuineness of your sessions. Another advantage is being able to enjoy each other fully without rigid expectations for what you can or cannot do. This means that at times—perhaps the majority of times—you may wish to include intercourse in your session. However, there may be times when one or both of you would like to experience the pleasurable feelings of manual, oral, or vibrator stimulation to orgasm. At times you may want to pleasure yourself in front of your partner or have your partner pleasure him or herself either as part of foreplay or as leading to orgasm.

For the women.   What would happen if you "let go" in front of your partner? Concerns about how your partner will respond when you experience orgasm may be causing you to stop yourself when you reach a certain level of arousal. You may find that at these times your mind wanders, other thoughts distract you, or your lose the good feelings that you were experiencing. Dealing with some of your worries will enable you to move past this point.

If you have not yet experienced orgasm, the first thing you should do is get in touch with some of your fears. Go back to Chapter 6 and re-read the section on "Role-Play Orgasm." Repeat this exercise during your next few individual sessions.

Can you verbalize some of your fears? Try sharing them with your partner, even if it seems a bit awkward. Reassurance and support are important for both of you at this point. For example, if arousal is accompanied by the feeling that you may urinate, share this fear with your partner. Your partner needs to know that it is not unusual for women to urinate a little during their first few orgasms, but control automatically develops fairly quickly. Discuss ways that you could handle this as a couple (keeping a towel near the bed) in the event that this happens.

The next step is to do the Role-Play Orgasm exercise during a few of your couple sessions. The first time you try this, each of you role-play having an exaggerated orgasm early in your session before you feel aroused. Do this one at a time so that the partner who is not role-playing can say or do some supportive things.

Saying things like "Go ahead," "Let go," "Come," or just being close and maintaining some contact—such as holding hands—can reassure and encourage your partner.

Repeat this again until you both feel you've really acted out some of your worst fears. You will probably find that you feel embarrassed and silly while doing this; that's all right. After a few times you both will probably be less concerned about letting go and enjoying what your body is feeling. The next time you find yourself "stuck" at a plateau of sexual arousal, try role-playing orgasm along with some of the orgasm triggers discussed in Chapter 6.

Something else which can interfere with your couple sessions are any uncomfortable or negative feelings you may have about your partner's genitals. Often women have these feelings because they are just unfamiliar with male anatomy.

Just as often, however, women's feelings regarding genitals may be related to negative attitudes about sex in general, or about men in particular, that were learned while growing up. For example, one woman being seen in sex therapy remembered first learning about conception at age 15, and was petrified by the idea of intercourse. The idea that a male's penis enters the woman's body was upsetting because she thought it would be painful. Also, because she was unfamiliar with male anatomy (she had never seen a male nude), she imagined a penis of enormous proportions. Before learning to pleasure her partner, this woman had to deal with her feelings about male genitals. We will discuss some ways to do this in a moment.

Of course, there are other ways in which women may learn to be sexually cautious of men. One woman we interviewed had a father who refused to let her date until her late teens. When she did begin to date, he constantly warned her to be on guard because "men are only interested in one thing." When this woman grew older she found that she couldn't relax and trust any man sexually. For her, men had become associated with distrust and possible harm. Our feelings about sex, then, are not something we are born with—we learn them from our experiences with our family and our friends; from things we read, see, or hear; and from the men we get to know. Feelings may be based on information given to us gradually (like parental attitudes) or on a particular experience (like rape). Since feelings about sexuality are learned, it is possible to unlearn them. So if you feel uncomfortable about the thought, sight, or touch of a man's genitals, you can, with time and an atmosphere of warmth and caring, learn to feel differently. Here are some suggestions to try. Some should be done with your partner. Others are best done on your own during your individual session.

1. Think about the sources from which you might have learned these feelings. Where did they come from? Do you ever remember feeling differently? What accounted for the change?

2. When you feel ready, talk about your feelings with your partner. Give him a chance to understand where your feelings are coming from. This will make it easier for him to give you encouragement, support, and the time to make changes. Changing patterns is a slow, uneven process. In return, it will be important for you to reassure your partner that your negative feelings do not stem from feelings about him as a person.

3. You may find looking at pictures of male genitals less uncomfortable than looking at the real thing. We suggest that you buy yourself a copy of one of the new women's magazines which feature nude males. These magazines are widely available in drugstores—you do not need to go to a pornography shop for them. You may be somewhat embarrassed to buy one of these magazines, but if you look inside the cover at the figures on the number of people who buy them, you'll find that you are not alone. These magazines will have lots of pictures of men, some of which show their genitals. Start slowly by paging through an issue until you find a picture that you like. Let your eyes linger over the body and face before looking at the genitals. Look at the genitals for as long as you're comfortable and then stop. Come back to the pictures a little longer each time until you feel you can look at pictures of male genitals without feeling uncomfortable.

4. If the last suggestion doesn't appeal to you, you may prefer to try an exercise that specifically includes your partner's genitals. Select a time when you are feeling pretty good about your partner (not when you've just had a disagreement, or when you are tired). You may like some kissing and caressing as you begin or you may not. Either way, communicate this to your partner.

The first time, just try looking at his genitals without touching them. If you are uncomfortable, you may want just to take a brief look and then continue touching and enjoying other parts of his body. Try this several times and gradually spend longer periods of time looking at his genitals. Talk to your partner about how easy or difficult it is for you—what you or he could do to make it easier.

When you can look at your partner's genitals comfortably, begin touching. The purpose is not for you to arouse your partner or even to give him pleasure. It is for you to learn about him through touching. Remember when you first began touching yourself? Try thinking of this as the same type of learning experience.

You may want your partner to lie still during this time and perhaps close his eyes so you won't feel that he is watching you. Make any suggestions that you feel will make you more relaxed and comfortable. Closing your own eyes for short periods while touching may help you tune into the feelings your hands and fingers are receiving. As you touch, try relating what you feel to other *good* touch sensations. For example: "The skin on this part of the penis is soft and smooth, almost silky." Also, try to compare the various textures of his genitals to other parts of his body—does the scrotal skin feel at all like the skin on his chest or abdomen? Does the penile skin around the glans feel like his lips? And finally, how do his genital textures compare to *your* own genitals? Notice similarities and differences and tell your partner what you are noticing.

5. The Name Game: Sexual words often carry positive or negative connotations and can relate to how you feel about your own and your partner's genitals. For one couple, for example,

"pussy" is usually used in a positive affectionate way, while "cunt" is harsher and more likely to be used when one partner is angry. Another couple may say "cunt" in a positive way when referring to female genitals. Playing this game with your partner can be fun as well as helping you feel more at ease using sexual words.

How to Play.   Each of you say out loud or make lists of all of the slang terms you know for the words below. You will want to share or list as many synonyms as you can think of:

Vagina	Testicles
Intercourse	Clitoris
Breasts	Menstruation
Penis	Ejaculation
Masturbation	Oral Genital Sex
(for men, for women)	(for men, for women)

After you've played (and hopefully exchanged a few laughs), try talking about which words on your lists you feel positively and negatively about. Can you help your partner understand what it is about the word and the image it produces that you like or that bothers you? As a couple, see if you can come up with your own vocabulary for communicating sexually which you both feel good about. You might even want to make "special" words of your own.

The purpose of this is to find sexual words which have *positive* meaning and image value for you. You may feel more comfortable thinking about or referring to your partner's penis, for example, as "dick" rather than as his "penis." Some couples even adopt affectionate nicknames for each other's genitals. If this is an idea you both like, try it!

6. Learning about male sexual anatomy and functioning will make your partner's body seem less frightening and foreign to you. For this reason we have included a drawing of male genitals that labels the various anatomical parts. We have also provided

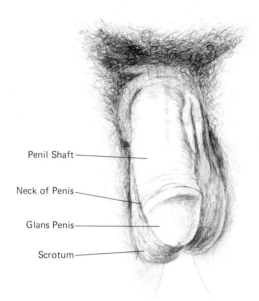

Penil Shaft

Neck of Penis

Glans Penis

Scrotum

you with drawings on the sequence of changes that occur during the male's sexual repsonse cycle. In order to make you feel better acquainted with what happens during male sexual arousal and orgasm, we would like to spend some time briefly describing some of the internal and external changes that take place.

As the male becomes aroused (*The Excitement Phase*) sexual tension increases blood flow to the pelvic area and penis and begins the process of penile erection. As the penis becomes erect it increases in length and diameter and the testes elevate. A smaller penis tends to increase more than a larger penis relative to its unstimulated size. Breathing becomes more rapid as heart rate increases. Some men experience nipple erection.

With greater arousal (*The Plateau Phase*), a flush may appear on the skin over certain areas of the body, blood pressure increases, and the penis usually becomes darker red with increased vasocongestion. Heart rate may increase over 100% of its normal pace. The testes elevate fully and increase in size while

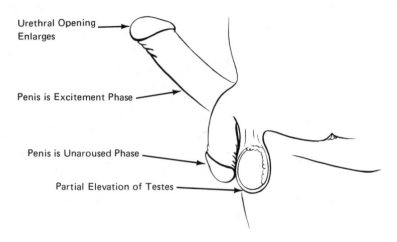

Urethral Opening
Enlarges

Penis is Excitement Phase

Penis is Unaroused Phase

Partial Elevation of Testes

UNAROUSED AND EXCITEMENT PHASES

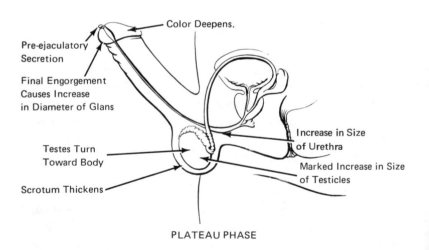

Color Deepens.

Pre-ejaculatory
Secretion

Final Engorgement
Causes Increase
in Diameter of Glans

Testes Turn
Toward Body

Scrotum Thickens

Increase in Size
of Urethra

Marked Increase in Size
of Testicles

PLATEAU PHASE

the skin of the scrotal sack (which supports the testes) thickens
somewhat. The glans of the penis enlarges, as does the urethral
opening and a small amount of seminal fluid may escape. This
pre-ejaculatory secretion often contains sperm. Just before
orgasm, there is a feeling of ejaculatory inevitability which
indicates the process of ejaculation has begun.

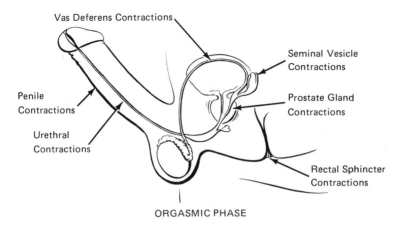

Vas Deferens Contractions

Seminal Vesicle
Contractions

Penile
Contractions

Prostate Gland
Contractions

Urethral
Contractions

Rectal Sphincter
Contractions

ORGASMIC PHASE

During orgasm (*The Orgasmic Phase*) contractions of a series of muscles propel seminal fluid out through the urethral opening. These contractions cannot be stopped once started.

After orgasm has occurred (*The Resolution Phase*), the penis quickly becomes less erect although full loss of erection often takes a while. Men vary in how quickly and completely they lose their erection after ejaculation. The testes descend and become smaller. The sex flush, heart rate and other changes return to their unstimulated state.

Overall, the phases of arousal and orgasm are very similar for men and women. The exception to these similarities are that the male ejaculates and almost always has a period following orgasm during which erection and/or orgasm are not possible. It is hoped that the information we've discussed about male sexual response will help you to feel more comfortable exploring your partner's body.

For the Man.   If you are learning to use an electric vibrator to pleasure your partner, you may have concerns about this. Some of these concerns were probably shared by your partner when she began using the vibrator herself. Reading Chapter 7 and talking with her may help reassure you.

However, often men have unique feelings about vibrators. You may worry that your partner will prefer this form of stimulation to anything which you could provide, or you may feel that using the vibrator is a reflection on your ability as a lover and be dismayed if your partner experiences orgasm for the first time while using the vibrator. You may feel detached from your partner while stimulating her with the vibrator, or feel used—as though you were nothing more than a "machine behind the machine."

All these feelings are natural and have occurred in other men. Your sexual education probably included the idea that *you* were responsible for how things went sexually with a woman. She may have controlled the limits, but you were responsible for "turning her on." If this was true for you, it may be hard for you to accept the use of the vibrator as a positive step.

Rather than seeing its use as a sign of failure, try seeing it as a convenience and a source of variety at this point. Right now, do what works! This will give you a firm base on which to expand and explore your growing sexuality as a couple. Here are some things which you and your partner can do to help incorporate vibrator stimulation into your sessions in a good way for both of you.

1. Let yourself get comfortable with the vibrator. Try using the vibrator on yourself, or have your partner use it on you over different parts of your body. Use it on your head, back, arms, legs, feet, and so on, as well as on your genitals. This will give you some idea how strong the vibrations are and also whether or not it provides you with pleasurable sensations. Most males enjoy some vibrator stimulation of their genitals, but it is important to learn where, how, and how much before you start teaching your partner.

2. Try to use a type of vibrator that you both enjoy. Chapter 7 illustrates and explains some types of vibrators that are available. Many men like the idea that their hand is on their partner's genitals, and you may find this is important to you both. If your partner has chosen a hand-held vibrator for her individual sessions, try using it to stimulate her. If you feel you would prefer the over-the-hand type, discuss this with your partner. You

might purchase one type and try it out. Leave the final decision, however, up to the woman. Some women have strong preferences. There is also no reason why (if you can afford it) you can't have two vibrators—one for the woman to use on herself and one for you to use on her. Try each one more than once since they take a while to learn to use with ease. Also, you should give some feedback on which type feels best on you.

3. Let the vibrator be an option, an enrichment to your sexual repertoire. This means that you won't necessarily use the vibrator each time you make love (although you may choose to do just that). By now you've learned a variety of ways to pleasure your partner. The vibrator can be thought of as an extension of yourself; by itself it is just an object, but used with care it is an instrument for pleasure. Keep the vibrator nearby (in a dresser or night-stand drawer or plugged in under the bed), so that getting at it isn't too distracting. Practice ways in which you both can initiate using it, for instance: "How about the vibrator now?" or "I'd like you to touch me with the vibrator." At times, though, you may want to stimulate your partner only with your hands or mouth and not use the vibrator. At other times you can alternate using the vibrator, your hands, and mouth in your lovemaking.

4. Do other stimulating things to your partner while using the vibrator. Kissing the woman's breasts while giving her genital stimulation can be extremely pleasurable. While using the vibrator on the male's penis, the woman could caress his testicles with her mouth or other hand. Let yourself be inventive! Reading Chapter 11 (Enrichment) may give you some ideas.

Sometimes during vibrator stimulation, watching your partner and gently encouraging her to get into her feelings may be all you want and need to do to feel like you are greatly involved in her pleasuring. The fact that you have provided an atmosphere of trust and caring that allows your partner to experience pleasure means a great deal. The vibrator cannot provide this atmosphere—it's you who helps make it possible.

It is not uncommon for women to have difficulty becoming

aroused through nonvibrator types of stimulation after they have learned to become aroused or orgasmic with a vibrator. This is not surprising, since vibrators provide intense stimulation. If, as a couple, you have had success achieving arousal or orgasm with vibrator stimulation of the woman, you may want to become more skillful at other kinds of stimulation, (see Chapter 11).

Here are some suggestions:

Try these suggestions after the woman finds it relatively easy to experience arousal with a vibrator in front of her partner. This is to make sure that you have overcome most of your inhibitions about showing arousal in front of each other.

1. Try alternating the vibrator with other forms of stimulation. Allow the woman to become highly aroused or close to orgasm and then begin vigorous manual or oral stimulation. This technique will take a lot of patience and practice to go smoothly. Since discontinuing one form of stimulation and beginning another may stop orgasm in the woman, you both have to expect some restimulation to be necessary and possibly some feelings of frustration to occur. Let her be the guide here on how many times she wants to try this technique in a given session. If the experience is to upsetting or too frustrating, discontinue it. Try it again at another time.

2. For some women, more stimulation after an orgasm feels extremely good. However, other women are extremely sensitive after an orgasm (particularly if a vibrator was used), and any additional stimulation is painful. If the woman is able to have an orgasm with the use of the vibrator she can try stimulating herself manually or having you stimulate her manually soon (30 seconds—two minutes) after orgasm. If the feelings are pleasant, it may be easier to produce arousal manually or orally at this time since the genitals will still be in an aroused state. Again, let the woman determine what should be done and for how long.

For You Both. At this stage, people often experience concerns about stimulating or pleasuring their partner or letting themselves be pleasured. You may feel that you or your partner require an undue amount of stimulation in order to feel pleasure, arousal, or orgasm. Women in particular tend to feel that they are "abnormal" because of the amount or kind of stimulation that they need. They may feel that they are being selfish and fear that their partner is feeling bored, detached, or resentful. Fears and worries of this kind can put tremendous strain on your sexual sessions. It can prevent you from feeling pleasure, and even from experiencing orgasm. Knowing what is "normal" for women helps to relieve many of these fears. From our experience in helping many women learn to have orgasms, we have noticed that when a woman first becomes orgasmic it is not unusual for her to want and need a good deal of time and stimulation—an hour is not unusual. When we say stimulation, we are including hugging, kissing, massage, breast and other body area pleasuring. Genital stimulation itself may vary from a few minutes to 45 minutes. (We are not including intercourse here. We will talk about intercourse in Chapter 10.)

Alternating among pleasuring, being pleasured, and mutual pleasuring will help insure that both of you are *involved* in what's happening. If all the attention is focused upon the woman to have orgasm, feelings of resentment and impatience on the male's part, and frustration and guilt on the female's part, are bound to occur. And, as we mentioned before, the pressure on both partners to perform makes pleasure impossible. Rather, try and focus in on your own pleasure and remember that you can't force orgasm to occur. Communication is crucial here. You both will want to make sure you are getting the kind of pleasurable stimulation that feels good to you. Also, at this stage, try to give lots of positive feedback to your partner. Usually feelings of boredom and detachment occur when one partner is feeling left out and unsure of what his or her partner is feeling. Giving reassurance to your partner may mean nothing more than a grunt or moan to indicate satisfaction. Saying a few words—such as "nice," "more" or "that feels so good"—also contributes to feelings of intimacy and involvement.

Earlier, we talked about arousal and orgasm as a natural response which many women have *learned* to ignore or suppress.

Throughout the exercises in this book, you (as individuals and as a couple) have been learning how to help your bodies experience these sensations. We like to view this knowledge as learned skills which you will improve, expand, and embellish upon with time and experience. As you become more comfortable and skillful with different forms of sexual pleasuring, it will become easier and easier to experience arousal.

Usually the more orgasms a woman has, the easier it is to have more. Why? No one is exactly sure. One physiological reason may be that stimulation that leads to arousal and orgasm increases the flow of blood to the genitals. Increased blood flow may result in additional small capillaries (vessels that carry blood) being formed. This additional blood supply may make it easier for blood to rush to the genitals and hence for pleasurable feelings to occur sooner. This process takes time, obviously, so don't be discouraged.

The important thing is to give yourselves time and lots of opportunities to learn. How much specifically genital and clitoral stimulation a woman wants and needs depends on the woman. Some men are surprised to find that the most pleasurable stimulation for their partner is a very repetitious continuous movement at some spot on the genitals—for example, a circular motion massaging on the side of the clitoris. If the movement is stopped, the building arousal often subsides. So don't be surprised if your partner is very choosy about what kind of stimulation he or she desires. You have learned a lot about yourselves— and for both of you this knowledge is just beginning to expand. Give yourselves the chance to teach each other about your needs and you will find it becomes easier for you to participate and to share in your partner's pleasure.

FANTASIES

Fantasy can also increase the pleasure you and your partner get out of your sexual experiences together. We already discussed fantasy in Chapter 5 as an aid to enhancing the woman's individual sessions. We hope that you have become somewhat more comfortable about the idea of fantasy as a way to expand and increase your sexual responsiveness. However, you may feel differently about using fantasy while having sex with a partner, in contrast to using it during masturbation.

Two particularly frequent areas of concern seem to be: 1) What does it mean about myself or my partner if I use fantasies during our lovemaking? and 2) How will using fantasy affect our sexual relationship? Some women feel that there is something wrong with them or with their sexual relationship if they imagine sex with someone other than their partner—"Shouldn't he be enough to turn me on?" Other people are concerned that they may only be able to become aroused through fantasy, that sex with their partner will be less satisfying than their imaginary sexual activities, and that eventually sex with their partner will not be satisfying at all. Actually, recent studies on female sexuality have shown that many (over 50%) married women do fantasize at least some of the time during sexual activities with their partner. Women who do fantasize also tend to have sexual daydreams—thoughts about sexual situations—at times when they are not actually doing anything sexual; and they are often imaginative and creative people. Most women who fantasize frequently enjoy their fantasies, and have what they describe as a satisfying sexual relationship with their partner.

Fantasy seems to give people the opportunity to enjoy thinking about having sex in a variety of different circumstances. Imagining ourselves in all sorts of sexual situations can be exciting and fun—just like imagining going on a world cruise might be fun. Also, many fantasies include activities that we would never really do. Such fantasies add interest and allow us to satisfy our curiosity, while still protecting ourselves (and other people) from doing something we really don't want to do.

Of course the content of fantasies varies a lot from person to person, as you can see from reading Nancy Friday's *My Secret Garden* or *Forbidden Flowers*. Some women remember past lovemaking scenes they have had. Some women include their sexual partner in their fantasies but change the place (to a beach, a car, a party, a shower, the desert, a cabin in the woods), change the number of other people present (ménage à trois, orgies, mate-swapping), or the kinds of activities (spanking, aggression, force, submission). Other women imagine these situations without including their partner in their fantasy.

In thinking about yourself, you may be concerned about the theme of your fantasies, or you may be concerned that you do not include your partner. One way in which you can deal with these feelings is to think about what good effects your fantasies have on you and your sexual relationship with your partner. For instance: 1) They may enhance your feelings of arousal and make you feel more sexual—the increased arousal is something that you do share with your partner and is something that he enjoys too; 2) fantasy can be another way of getting in a sexual mood and focusing on sex rather than worrying about what happened during your day or how much you have to do tomorrow; and 3) your fantasies are another way you can take responsibility for letting yourself become aroused rather than expecting your partner to do everything to turn you on physically *and* mentally.

Fantasies are not reality. Fantasies are part of your personal sexual expression. If they include some activity like whipping or orgies, you may never really want to act them out, but you may just like and find exciting the forbidden quality of certain sexual scenes. Remember that as we were growing up and discovering what sexuality meant, the whole idea of sex was taught to be somewhat forbidden. So it's not surprising that some of us want to retain that element of intrigue. However, you may be able to include some parts of your fantasies in your lovemaking. You might look at Alex Comfort's *Joy of Sex* to get ideas for how to do this in a fun and loving way.

Another way you can deal with your negative feelings about fantasy is to try discussing some of these feelings with your partner. You may want to try telling one of your fantasies to your partner and have him do the same. Some couples also like to try constructing a joint fantasy—a kind of erotic story—just to see what they can put together. These are both ways of sharing and getting more comfortable with the idea of having fantasies in the presence of your partner. Alternatively, you may decide *not* to share your fantasies. Often the secretiveness of the fantasy is what makes it special—if this is true for you, it's fine to keep it for yourself. What is important is to communicate to your partner your mutual acceptance of the fantasy side of his/her sexuality, to reassure them that fantasy enhances your sexuality and therefore is likely to continue having a positive influence on your growing sexuality as a couple.

In sharing fantasy, one common issue is concern over your partner fantasizing about someone else. While most people aren't too upset by their partner having sexual fantasies about a movie star or magazine centerfold, many people are worried, jealous, or upset to hear that his/her partner has sexual fantasies about someone you actually know personally. If you have such fantasies, you may not want to share them with your partner, but keep them as your own private fantasies. If you do share them with your partner, make it clear that these are just fantasies, that you are not going to act on them. You should both remember that it is normal to be sexually attracted to other people. Such attraction does not mean that you are not attracted to your partner, nor does it mean that you are promiscuous or likely to act out the fantasy.

Remember, too, that if you don't fantasize during sex, and don't particularly want to, that's fine, too. Just focusing on your physical enjoyment and your partner's enjoyment can be equally pleasurable, as long as it's satisfying for you.

WHAT'S NATURAL FOR YOU

It is very important for you both to give yourselves time and to accept whatever your sexual needs and desires are. Comparing yourselves to others is self-defeating. The idea of sexual growth implies a variety of means and ways to grow. If arousal and orgasm are only possible through the strong rapid motion of a vibrator, then that is what's *right* and *natural* for you right now. Given time, your needs and desires may change; but let it be a natural change, rather than a change due to insecurities and pressures about what *should* happen.

10

Intercourse—
Another Form
of Mutual Pleasure

Often when we hear the word "sex" we automatically assume that sexual intercourse or coitus is being discussed. One reason for this is that intercourse seems to play an extremely important part in our sexuality.

Certainly, in terms of biology, this is true: Conception of children almost always involves intercourse. The significance of conception and the responsibilities of parenthood set intercourse apart from other sexual activities. Partly for this reason, regulations concerning intercourse are included in moral, religious, and legal standards governing sex. These standards emphasize the importance of intercourse and generally restrict, at least in our culture, its occurrence to marriage. Because of this, many of us have learned to feel that intercourse is better than other forms of sexual expression and that once we are

married or involved in a loving relationship, all sexual encounters should end with intercourse.

These kinds of feelings can influence your sexual growth in
many ways. For example, you may not feel free to explore a full
range of sexual activities if you or your partner believe that you
must have intercourse every time you have sex. Foreplay under
these conditions may become perfunctory—a brief preliminary
that automatically precedes intercourse rather than a pleasure of
its own.

Similarly, you may feel guilty about those times when you
cannot or don't want to have intercourse. Intercourse may not
be desired, for instance, during the woman's menstrual period,
during a vaginal infection, when the man has difficulty getting
and maintaining an erection, or when one partner is tired. Since
other activities are seen as second best, resentments and feelings
of frustration often develop.

Another problem that can result from overemphasizing intercourse is the tendency to judge your sexual relationship and
your sexual competency on the basis of what happens during
intercourse. We have seen couples who feel there is something
desperately wrong with them if intercourse is not as enjoyable
for them as manual stimulation. Some of the women we see are
orgasmic through self-stimulation, and through manual and
sometimes oral stimulation by their partner, but not during
intercourse. Rather than seeing arousal and orgasm during
intercourse as another skill that people learn, the man or woman
may believe that lack of coital orgasm is a symptom of an
emotional or physical problem. This leads to all kinds of concerns about such things as penis size (too large, too small), size
of the vagina (too tight, too loose), size of the clitoris and hood
(too large, too small, too tight), as well as doubts about the
relationship itself, and about yourself as a person (does this
mean that you can't give love?).

Sitting down with your partner and trying to sort out your
feelings is a first step. Once you're in touch with how you feel
and what your beliefs or expectations are about intercourse,

you'll be in a better position to make those changes which will contribute to positive sexual growth as a couple.

Here are some questions to consider when sharing your feelings together.

1. Is either of you dissatisfied if a sexual encounter doesn't include intercourse? Why? Where do your feelings come from? (Where and how did you learn to feel the way you do?)

2. What else beside genital sensations is pleasurable for you both during intercourse? For instance, do you feel emotionally closer?

3. Is it very important for you both that the male partner ejaculate during intercourse? What if ejaculation occurs during some other activity, such as oral or manual pleasuring or not at all? How does this change the experience for you?

4. If the woman experiences orgasm before or after, rather than during intercourse, how does this make each of you feel?

Perhaps in discussing the above questions together you found that you and your partner were more flexible than you had thought. You may both be willing to re-evaluate your feelings about intercourse and orgasm during intercourse. You might try having a few sessions that exclude intercourse entirely and see what you can discover about other erotic pleasures. Or you might have intercourse in the middle of a session and then go on to orgasm through another form of stimulation. One advantage of these alternatives is that they reduce feelings of pressure to have orgasm during intercourse and allow you to make the experience slow and sensual. Alternating sensual movement with no movement, and really focusing in on the warm sensations of physical closeness can enrich your sexual communication. Give yourself the chance to experience intercourse as a form of lovemaking that has special qualities of its own. Intercourse need not be a race to orgasm, nor a requirement for you to feel good about yourself, your partner, and your sexuality.

Perhaps one of you prefers intercourse more than your

partner. Often, the male finds intercourse somewhat more stimulating than the female (we will talk about this more fully in a moment). There are other reasons too—one being the long-standing feeling that intercourse *is* the most important activity and makes sex really SEX. What we ask you to think about, if this is your feeling, is that sex is usually more than just genital stimulation: Through sex you express your pleasure of another person, your caring for him/her, your concern, and your desire to share intimacy and affection. Since sex involves both of you, you must be sensitive to giving in a way that your partner can appreciate. This means being attuned to what the other person would like. Each of you will probably want to experience some activities that are more stimulating for your partner (intercourse may be one of these) than for yourself; at other times you may decide on something that is more stimulating to you. Other activities will be equally pleasurable for both of you.

When you have learned something about your own body and your partner's body, and when you have learned ways to communicate those discoveries to each other, you are ready to integrate intercourse into your sessions as another natural and loving activity for giving each other pleasure. To do this, you may need to learn new ways to make intercourse as pleasing as possible for each of you so that you can really share equally in the experience. It may sound simple, but sexual communication is as complex as the changing needs of the people involved. You will find it takes patience and consideration and the expectation that it does *not* happen automatically.

Start by looking at where you are now. You may have experienced orgasm, either through your own stimulation, your partner's stimulation, or both. If you haven't yet had an orgasm, this does not mean that something is "wrong" with you. It may mean that you need to spend more time practicing on earlier steps. If you are getting aroused at least some of the time, then you are on your way.

If you find that you're getting more aroused in your mutual pleasuring than in your self-pleasuring sessions, then you may want to spend more time in your mutual sessions. If your individual sessions seem to be going better than those with your partner, you might want to slow down on your partner sessions to concentrate on making progress alone. Different women make progress in different ways: Some women find that becoming aroused is easier when they are alone because they feel less distracted and more able to concentrate on themselves; other women find that their partner's presence enhances their own ability to become aroused.

We recommend that you wait to do this step until you are feeling at least some arousal during either your individual or couple sessions with your partner. It is not necessary for you to have had an orgasm. However, if *you* feel you would not like to try intercourse without first feeling more aroused or experiencing orgasm, that's fine too. Discuss these feelings with your partner.

Before we describe what we would like you to try, we want to share with you some feelings and concerns that other couples have had at this point. Read through them; and if any are particularly relevant to either or both of you, it will help your sessions if you talk about your reactions:

Unhappy Memories. At times, one or both partners feel nervous about trying new things during intercourse because of unsatisfying or frustrating experiences that have happened in the past. In these cases, intercourse was usually accompanied by pressure to perform. You may have felt criticized in the past for not reaching orgasm; your partner may have felt similarly if he ejaculated too fast or too slowly. Resentment, feelings of failure, and disappointment usually grow naturally out of such situations. If you have unhappy memories, it will be very important to reassure each other that you are going to try not to let these situations repeat themselves. Sharing your feelings and taking any pressure for orgasm off each other will help.

He/She Will Never Really Change. Some changes in the area of sex will be easy for you to make. Sometimes, however, partners realize that there are some areas in which they are unwilling, or find it difficult, to change. If the particular issue is rather small, sometimes the other partner can just accept the difference and not let it interfere with more important concerns. However, if you reach a stalemate on a major issue, one in which no giving-in or compromising is possible, it may prevent you from even trying to work together sexually. If talking about it does not seem to help, let us make a few general suggestions that can apply to changes you want to make in any area of your life.

1. Be specific about the changes that need to be made. For example, say: "I would like it if you initiated sex a couple of times this week" rather than, "I would like you to be more enthused about sex."

2. Rather than attack the problem as a whole, you could try compromising on one small aspect of it. People find it very tempting to try to overcome a difficulty as completely and quickly as possible; and sometimes there is too much to solve all at once. It's best to start with a small change which your partner feels he/she will be able to make rather than to expect drastic changes overnight. Starting small also makes it more likely that you will succeed rather than disappoint each other. An example of this would be: "I'd really like you to kiss me more during foreplay" rather than "I'd like it if you'd be more romantic."

3. First work on those areas where you and your partner both agree that there is a need for change. This, again, makes it more likely that you will succeed since you are both interested in making the changes.

4. Share what each of you finds rewarding or pleasurable; and show your interest and enthusiasm about any progress that is made toward the changes you desire. This is extremely important. You have no doubt experienced discouragement and felt like giving up when efforts you were making went unrecognized. Recognizing and rewarding another person's efforts to change is one of the best ways to show your appreciation and to insure that they continue to improve.

Throughout our lives, appreciation is shown to us in different ways. As kids, we might get a pat on the head, a hug, a "that's great," money, or even a gold star. As adults, too, both material (a gift, money) and non-material (a touch, words, a smile) acknowledgment can be very rewarding. Sometimes just hearing someone say, "That really means a lot to me" can make us feel tremendously appreciated. It's important to acknowledge *any* effort toward change, because it will help encourage the person making the change. Of course you need to know what meaningful forms of appreciation are for each of you. Two people often differ on how they would like their partner to acknowledge and reward their efforts. For example, a man may find it very rewarding to have his partner say that she loves him. However, a more meaningful way of his communicating appreciation for *her* might be through actions rather than words. For example, his putting the children to sleep or spontaneously suggesting a night out may be far more rewarding to her than a verbal statement of love. You both should talk over what are the important ways your partner can show his/her appreciation toward you.

5. Both of you have a responsibility to try to make the changes in your own behavior that your partner wants. Sometimes this is difficult, and a couple may get caught up in the issue of who's going to change first. Rather than either partner taking a risk and feeling vulnerable, they may find themselves engaged in a power struggle while the situation remains the same. To help to avoid this problem, it helps for *both* partners to agree to work on some changes *each* needs to make. You will probably find that your partner is more willing to work hard at changing in ways you consider important, if at the same time you are working hard at making the changes he/she wants.

If you hit an obstacle in an area where you disagree about the need for change, consider the reasons why one of you doesn't want to change. Patterns sometimes feel safe even if they are harmful. Are you afraid of what might happen if you do change? Or what your partner's response might be? In what specific ways do you think your partner may be making it difficult for you to change? How could he/she make it easier? Try discussing the situation from this perspective and see if you can make some headway. If you are not able to get anywhere at all, you may want to consider some intensive sex or marriage therapy to deal with this area of your relationship. We will talk about ways to seek outside help in Chapter 12.

Physical Concerns and Problems. A frequent worry of men, at some stage in their development, is that their penis is too small. Less frequently, but often enough, women mention that they think their vagina may be too large or too small. Genital size does vary among individuals, but it should not influence a person's ability to experience arousal or to arouse his/her partner.

If you go back and look at the drawings in Chapter 2 showing the female sexual response cycle, you will see that the vagina is actually a sort of closed organ. When the penis enters the vagina, the vagina accomodates to the size and shape of the penis. Women can also learn to contract their vaginal muscles to provide maximum contact between the penis and vagina (Kegel exercises). Only about the first third of the vagina is sensitive to touch, the back part being almost totally insensitive. Most of the stimulation for the woman during intercourse comes from stimulation of the clitoris, either directly through touching or indirectly through pulling on the vaginal lips during thrusting. It is not necessary to have deep penetration during intercourse for the woman to experience pleasure or orgasm. Other pleasurable feelings may come from full body contact, from feelings of pressure or of fullness in the vagina, from contact between the head of the penis and the cervix (although some women find this uncomfortable), and, of course, from the sight, smell, and sounds of their partner. Also, variations in position produce sensations by providing deep or shallow penetration of the vagina (see pages 170–176).

It is not necessary, then, that the male have a particular size or shape of penis, or the woman a particular size or shape of vagina, in order to experience pleasure and arousal. Pleasure and stimulation depend on what you do and feel for each other, not on the size of your sexual equipment. It is possible, of course, that size might be a psychological turn-on for someone, but that alone is not sufficient for a good sexual experience.

Another fairly common concern of women is the occasional experience of some sort of pain or discomfort during intercourse. This can be caused by a variety of things. Certain positions for intercourse are sometimes uncomfortable because of the angle or depth of penile thrusts. A urinary or vaginal infection can cause irritation or burning sensations during or after intercourse. If you think this might be the case, you should see your physician or gynecologist.

If you are tense during sex, your vaginal muscles may be somewhat tight and make penetration uncomfortable. More practice in general relaxation usually helps. Having a relaxation session before your couple sessions is something you might try. Continuing with your Kegel exercises will also give you more control over your vaginal muscles. It will make it easier for you to relax these muscles, just as you learned to relax the rest of your body. If at the time of penetration you feel tense, try a few Kegels and then guide the penis into your vagina when you feel your muscles are more relaxed. You should guide the penis into your vagina slowly. Some women find that a slight baring-down of their vaginal muscles during insertion helps because it prevents them from tightening up, since it is impossible to do both at the same time.

Also, find some positions for insertion that make this step easier. You may want to insert the penis while you're in one position (female on top for example), and then maneuver yourselves into another position before beginning intercourse movements. This takes practice, so expect to feel clumsy and awkward for a while. Finally, a lack of lubrication can cause a lot of irritation—try using K-Y jelly or Lubrifax on both the penis and the vaginal opening. If slow, relaxing foreplay, penetration, and discussion with your partner does not help your discomfort, you should see a physician who can treat you or refer you for sex therapy.

ENJOYING INTERCOURSE

It is not unusual for a man to get more enjoyment from intercourse than a woman. This varies with the couple, how well their bodies "fit" together, and the position that is used for intercourse. The penis is usually receiving direct stimulation, while stimulation to the clitoris may be very indirect. For some women, indirect stimulation of the clitoris during intercourse is sufficient for becoming aroused and experiencing orgasms. However, in order to experience sexual arousal and orgasm, many women need some additional manual or vibrator stimulation to their clitoral area during intercourse.

Even though many women need this extra stimulation during intercourse, there is a strong tendency for them, and often for their partners, to feel that this is abnormal or wrong. If you have these feelings, think about them for a moment, consider where you might have developed them, and see if you can put them in a slightly different perspective. We would like to mention a few facts that should help you begin to re-evaluate at your ideas.

First, most women are taught that the vagina is their primary sexual organ, and that it is the greatest source of sexual pleasure. Women in our society often do not know what a clitoris is, where their clitoris is, or why they have one, until long after they have learned about their vaginas. So, even though the clitoris is far more sensitive than the vagina, its presence tends to be ignored as a woman develops sexually. The message we can easily get from this is that the clitoris is or should be unimportant to good sex, and that if we like the feelings we get there, something is strange about us.

Keep in mind that in desiring clitorial stimulation during lovemaking, you are asking for the same kind of stimulation that provides your male partner with sexual pleasure—during intercourse he receives direct stimulation to the sensitive glans area of his penis. It makes sense that you should be able to experience direct stimulation of your clitoral glans also.

At those times when you don't desire additional stimulation during intercourse, it's a good idea to allow yourself to get quite highly aroused before penetration takes place. Also, it is very important here for the woman to let her partner know (verbally or nonverbally) when she should like him to enter her, and how hard or rapidly he should thrust to maintain her arousal. (Some ways to prolong intercourse will be discussed in Chapter 11.) One way that many couples use to trigger orgasm during intercourse is this: After the woman becomes very aroused—almost to the point of orgasm—the male begins either very rapid or very strong and deep thrusting. The woman can use her hands to guide the pace and depth of her partner's movements.

If you still feel restricted by always needing manual or vibrator stimulation during intercourse, you might try the following suggestions:

1. As we mentioned above, let yourself become very aroused with other forms of stimulation (manual, oral or masturbation), and after intromission, guide or let your partner know what kinds of thrusting feel best. Use a position that allows you to use your arms to guide his thrusting, as well as one that allows you to move your hips to adjust the tempo and the pressure to your needs. You may initially lose *some* of your arousal during the few moments you change to intercourse stimulation. Don't be concerned about this because once you have reached and remain at a fairly high level of arousal for a short time, your body takes quite a while (anywhere from five minutes to an hour or more) to return to where it was before arousal. So it may *feel* like you've "lost it," but actually your body is still aroused.

2. Another variation of "blending" into intercourse stimula-

tion alone for you to reach a high level of arousal during intercourse with the additional clitoral stimulation you need. When you are highly aroused, and very close to orgasm (with time you will be able to know this), discontinue the additional stimulation and, again, guide your partner's thrusts to provide you with the best stimulation. If this works for you, over the various times when you have intercourse, let the time at which you stop the additional stimulation gradually become earlier and earlier during your arousal. You may be able to eventually learn to get more pleasure from intercourse without simultaneous manual or vibrator stimulation, although you probably will always enjoy and need some direct clitoral stimulation prior to intercourse.

3. Whatever you decide to do, these changes take time, lots of patience, and a good deal of cooperation from your partner. It's important that he understands the necessity of you guiding him. If you try this, make sure he reads this section and you both talk over your concerns before a session, and your reactions afterwards.

Remember that you do not *have* to have additional clitoral stimulation during intercourse—some women do find that indirect stimulation is more pleasurable. Also, at times you may be more sensitive or less sensitive around your clitoris and vaginal opening (for example, at certain times in your menstrual cycle). You may find that you like a slightly different pressure or stroke for maximal stimulation at these times. Don't expect your partner to know automatically what feels good. By guiding him and using verbal and nonverbal communication you can let him know when you are experiencing pleasure.

Another expectation that many couples have is that they should experience their orgasms at the same time. Simultaneous orgasm occurs more often with some couples than others, but it rarely happens regularly. It would be unrealistic at this time for you to expect simultaneous orgasms—in fact it might even be detrimental to your sexual expression. Why? Because again, this would put pressure on you and your partner to "go after" orgasm instead of just enjoying pleasurable feelings. The pressure would be on both of you to hold back or speed up. By doing this you would be actually distracting yourself from experiencing the natural buildup of erotic pleasure you could be experiencing. You would also be putting more emphasis on orgasm than on your own or your partner's enjoyment, and might miss many of the rich erotic sensations that lead to orgasm. For the woman in particular, emphasizing the timing of orgasm may actually prevent her from reaching satisfaction.

We are not trying to play down the delights of simultaneous orgasm. We are just suggesting that they not be sought as the ultimate sexual experience. With this in mind, you can enjoy this when it occurs, but not be disappointed or inhibit other aspects of your lovemaking if it doesn't. Also, having your partner experience his/her orgasm separately from your own has its own rewards—it allows you to appreciate their personal orgasmic expression far more completely. Feeling sexual excitement build in your body, hearing his/her sounds, being physically and emotionally close at the moment of his/her orgasm can be a very special and intimate experience of its own.

YOUR SESSIONS

As you begin, we would like you to just get comfortable with each other and do whatever is pleasurable for you both (for now, be guided by the woman's preferences). This may include some talking, mutual massage, cuddling, kissing, stroking, or whatever else you like. If you have found the vibrator enjoyable, it too can be included in some general body stimulation. This period of time is very important both to set a comfortable atmosphere and to be sensual, to be affectionate, and along the way, to become aroused. You should not rush foreplay: Let it go on for as much time as you like—an hour is not too long. It depends on you both. For now, let the woman decide when to begin intercourse. Feeling "ready" might depend upon how aroused you are or how lubricated you are—but you do not have to be either highly aroused or very wet around your genital area. Just wait until you *want* to begin intercourse.

It is important at first for you (the woman) to guide the entry of the penis into your vagina. If you are not lubricated enough for the penis to enter comfortably, you may use some K–Y jelly and smooth it over your partner's penis and inside of your vagina (you can make this fun and stimulating with a little practice). When the penis is inside your vagina, don't feel like you have to rush into rapid thrusting. Take your time.

At first you can try just lying together without moving at all while the penis is contained vaginally. During this time, you can talk or stroke other parts of each other's bodies. Try a few vaginal squeezes around the penis and see if your partner can feel them. For a while you might try caressing each other's genitals with your hands: The clitoris, breasts, and testicles will probably all be within reach. As you do begin to move, try slow gentle body movement at first. The woman should guide the extent of pelvic thrusting and tell her partner so that you both learn how *deep* the penis can go without hurting, how *rapid* the rhythm of movements should be, and *how long* thrusting should continue. There is no way for one partner to be able to *know* these things without the other partner's verbal or nonverbal guidance. You will find that your preferences will differ at different times and in different positions—so you must involve your partner and indicate to him what feels good and what doesn't.

At the same time that you are having intercourse, it is important for your partner or yourself to be stimulating your genital area. He may do this either manually or with a vibrator, depending on what works best for you (try both eventually). Remember to let your feelings flow and to guide his hand or give him feedback, just as you have done earlier.

If you have not tried intercourse with manual stimulation before, you will find this awkward at first. Learning to arrange

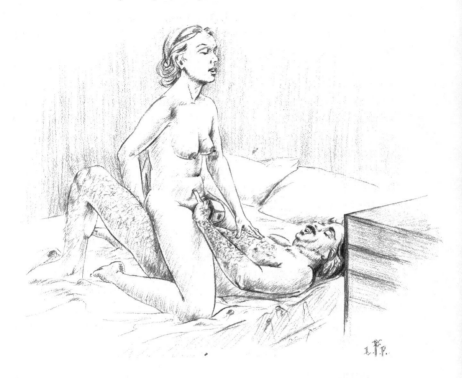

bodies and arms and hands takes a while. There are several positions that will make this easier and that other people have found are fun. Each position has special satisfactions—discover the ones that best meet your mutual needs and desires.

One position is when the woman is *astride and on top* of the man as he is lying on his back. This gives the man access to the woman's breasts and genitals while she is able to stimulate his chest, thighs, and testicles as well. This position gives you both a good opportunity to talk and look at each other while you are caressing each other. Hugging and kissing is more difficult, since the woman is in a seated position. One of the most important benefits of the woman being in this position is that it allows her freedom to move around during intercourse—something that is more difficult when her partner is on top of her. She can easily guide the penis into her vagina, control how quickly and deeply the penis enters, and direct the tempo of thrusting. If your male partner becomes very quickly aroused and you both want to delay his ejaculation, you can just slip the penis out of your vagina, and continue non-genital caressing until he is ready to begin intercourse again. Another possibility is to just pause and remain still with the penis inside the vagina. It is important here for the man to be able to judge when stimulation needs to be stopped or slowed down. Once the urge to ejaculate is felt it is too late to stop the ejaculatory reflex. Experience is the best teacher for this—expect that while you are practicing there will be times when ejaculation will occur too quickly. Chapter 11 gives more detail on ways to increase ejaculatory control.

Another situation is also not uncommon: If he loses his erection, you can take the penis from your vagina and resume pleasuring genital and non-genital areas until you desire to insert the penis again. If his penis remains erect during intercourse but still slips out of your vagina, don't worry about it: Just guide it back inside, or, while the penis is slippery, just try rubbing your labia and clitoris along the length of his penis for some extra stimulation.

Another position is one we call the *spoons* position—where both people lie on their side with the woman's back against the man's chest. Although this position does not allow you to look at each other, it does provide the man with easy access to the woman's genitals, breasts, and kissing or oral caresses around her neck and shoulders. It also can be a very cuddly position and provide feelings of closeness for you both. This is a good position for using the vibrator, too. When his hand is touching your genitals, you can put your hand over his, as you have done before, to adjust the tempo and pressure of his touch (see p. 173).

In what is unromantically known as the *lateral position,* the couple faces each other while on their sides. Your legs intertwine like scissors, and you will have to adjust yourselves in order to find a comfortable way for the vagina to hold the penis. Once you figure that out, this position allows you to do a lot of dif-

ferent kinds of pleasuring. Since neither of you is supporting the other person's weight, you have freedom to touch and stroke other person's weight, you have freedom to mutually touch and stroke each other all over the face, upper body, genitals, and can do it together, although the woman should, for now particularly, direct it more so that she doesn't feel rushed or uncomfortable. This is a fun part of this position, since you will have a chance to wiggle around and laugh at yourselves when the penis (as it is likely to do at first) slips out. Once you begin moving and thrusting, you may want to hold onto each other's buttocks —this helps to keep the penis in place and provides some pressure to the genital area that both partners usually like. However, the woman is likely to need more clitoral touching, too, so the man should also try different ways of touching her genitals during intercourse in this position.

A *rear entry* position, with the male entering the female from behind while she is on her knees, is a good position for genital stimulation for the woman, as the man can reach around her hips and touch her clitoris easily. This position is surrounded by a number of sexual myths. One is that this is a more "animalistic" than human position, because many animals have coitus in this way. A better way to look at this position is that it provides another opportunity to share different kinds of pleasurable feelings. Some cultures, Sweden for instance, regard rear entry as one of the more preferred positions. Another myth about this position is that it is a homosexual pattern. Homosexuals (males) as well as heterosexuals actually practice *anal* intercourse in which the penis is contained in the anus. Although anal intercourse can also be stimulating and enjoyable, and is used by many heterosexual couples, it is *not* the same as rear entry into the vagina.

The rear entry position allows for extra penile depth (so go slowly at first!) plus buttock stimulation and easy access to the female's breasts and clitoris. Also, many men find the rear view of their partner to be an added pleasure (notice how the spoons position is a variation of rear entry). Rear entry can be done in several ways. The two most common ways are: 1) The woman supports herself on her knees and hands while the male kneels and enters from behind. His hands are free to clasp her thighs and hips or to caress her breasts and clitoris. Or 2) the woman can rest her upper body on the edge of a bed or couch and kneel on the floor (use a pillow to make her knees comfortable). The male enteres from a kneeling or squatting position. Although rear entry does not allow the woman as much total body movement as some of the other positions, it does allow her to move her hips freely and to receive a good deal of manual stimulation to her clitoris. If you are hesitant about trying this, or any of the other positions, remember to share your reservations with your partner. Try making suggestions that might reduce your negative feelings, so that at least you feel comfortable exploring new forms of stimulation with each other.

And finally, there is the old favorite, the *man on top position.* It has attracted a variety of nicknames over the years, including "missionary," "matrimonial," and "Adam and Eve." This position seems to be one that a majority of couples include in their lovemaking a great deal of the time. It has some unique advantages. It provides a great deal of full body contact, and plenty of opportunity to hug, kiss, and nuzzle throughout your lovemaking. Some women like the feeling of a man's weight (but not all of it usually) pressing against them. The stimulation from his pelvic thrusting, however, may or may not be enough to highly arouse the woman. As a couple, you should explore different ways to continue caressing the clitoris during the time that the penis is in the vagina. Clitoral stroking is a bit more difficult for the male to maneuver in this position, but it can be done by his supporting himself on one elbow or arm, and will become less awkward with practice. At some point during clitoral stimulation, the woman may want just pelvic thrusting movements. Or she may want to continue with direct clitoral stimulation.

Communication is especially important in this position. The man actually has more physical control of thrusting and movement, so in order to make the experience as mutual as possible, the woman must express her needs and he must be tuned into her signals. This can make the difference between a frustrating and satisfying lovemaking experience. Keep in mind that one day is not the same as the next: Sexual needs and desires vary, so don't expect a particularly enjoyable pattern to be enjoyable forever after.

There are many variations that may help make this position more arousing for you. Placing pillows under the woman's buttocks may allow her to receive added clitoral stimulation from thrusting. The woman can vary the position of her legs to be open or to be closed tightly so the penis gets additional stimulation. And if she want to move a lot, he can support himself with his arms so that his pelvis is in a position and she can rise up to meet him. You can help control each other's thrusting by gripping each other's buttocks. And remember, this is not a "look, no hands" position. In addition to pelvic movements, almost everyone likes kissing and caressing over the rest of his/her body. Some people like to say sexual words or just make noise. Since this is a position you have probably tried, before you try it again, talk to each other about what you like and dislike about it. What changes would you like to make? How do you feel about trying extra clitoral stimulation in this position?

BEFORE YOU BEGIN

We suggest that before you actually use these positions in a session, you have some fun just trying each of them for practice and seeing which ones seem most interesting and comfortable for you. This will also help reduce the awkwardness of finding out where arms and legs have to go. Don't forget to discuss reservations you might have about certain positions—you won't enjoy trying if you feel like you have to just grin and bear it.

Don't feel confined to using only these positions. Your body shapes and your preferences may be suited to other variations. You might want to look at Alex Comfort's book, *The Joy of Sex,* to give you some more ideas. Feel free to invent your own style. The important thing to remember is to accompany penile stimulation with manual stimulation, depending, of course, on your particular needs.

Give yourselves 4 or 5 sessions to explore positions for pleasurable stimulation. During each session, we would like you to take your time and not feel rushed. After insertion, try just lying together without moving for a few moments while the penis is in the vagina; then try slow, gentle body movement for a while before you build up to more rapid, powerful stimulation. Depending on your position, slow shallow thrusting, deep strong thrusting, or sensuous circular pelvic movements may give the most pleasure. Try to focus in on what you are feeling rather than worrying about "how you are doing." Give positive verbal and nonverbal communication about what you like, keep tuned into each other's signals, and ask each other what feels good. Remember, this is exploration. Try each position on several different occasions—as you become more comfortable, you will discover new things about each other.

A lot of couples assume that once intercourse begins, it must continue until one or both partners have an orgasm. This doesn't have to be the case: You can have intercourse in the middle of your session and then try manual, vibrator, or oral genital stimulation; or you just hug and tumble around and then go back to intercourse. Intercourse, as we mentioned earlier, does not have to be the last activity you do together. For a change, you might want to end with manual or oral genital stimulation, or with each of you stimulating yourselves. Treating intercourse as another form of stimulation will help add variety and pleasure to your sessions. Viewing intercourse in this way will also help take pressure off both of you to get aroused and have orgasms through intercourse.

If you have been orgasmic in masturbation, see if you can let yourself have an orgasm with your partner. This may or may not happen easily. The best thing to do is not to get discouraged if progress is slow. Instead, try and concentrate on the small gains, the little improvements that you make each time you are together. All of the things you have learned about yourself and your partner are important. Try the orgasm triggers if you find yourself getting very aroused, but can't "let go." At times you may fantasize and lose yourself in yourself for a while. Don't feel responsible for your partner's pleasure so that you are afraid to let yourself fully experience your own. Remember that he is probably getting pleasure from your experience, and that at other times he too will lose himself in his own feelings.

AFTERWARD

The "afterplay" following each intercourse sessions is also an important part of lovemaking. What happens at this time may vary, depending upon whether you have had an orgasm or not, and depending on your mood.

At times you may want to enjoy the sensations of intercourse, but withdraw after a while and come to orgasm manually or with the stimulation of a vibrator. If the woman is multiply orgasmic, the man may want to give her some additional manual or oral stimulation after intercourse to make a second orgasm possible.

Often, you may want to just cuddle and talk or lie quietly and stroke each other before going to sleep. Try and become sensitive to your partner's mood during this time. Lots of hurt feelings have been caused by one partner turning over and going to sleep immediately after intercourse. Find out what your partner would like so that you can share this time as part of lovemaking.

11

Enhancement

When we say "enhancement," we are talking about the expansion of your sexuality to include new dimensions. For some people, enhancement may mean trying new intercourse positions, exploring different, non-intercourse activities, acting out some fantasies, or having sex at a different place and time. For other people, new partners, group sex, or swapping partners may be the directions they choose for enhancing their sexuality. What we would like to do in this chapter is mention a few basic guidelines for expanding your sexuality in ways that are not hurtful or destructive. We will also mention specific activities that many couples are curious about but which they may find difficult or upsetting to actually try.

One general guideline is that, usually, new sexual activities that directly involve another person *should not be tried at the expense of their fear or discomfort.* Force—in the form of a demand, a complaint, or sometimes a joking remark—generally has a negative effect on a person's overall enjoyment. This is not true under certain circumstances, such as both partners acknowledging that a certain amount of force is part of sex play.

If it does turn out that one partner is uncomfortable about trying a particular activity, try to figure out what about it is upsetting. Then, and this may be thought of as another guideline, *think of, and talk over ways that might gradually help the person learn to enjoy trying this new area of exploration.* For instance, a woman may be afraid of having oral-genital sex with her partner because she does not want him to ejaculate into her mouth. This concern is a common one, and there are several ways to deal with it. One is to talk over and agree on some kind of signal for the man to let the woman know when he feels orgasm starting. The signal can be a touch, a sound, or anything that's comfortable, natural, and clear enough to understand.

Another guideline to keep in mind is that *you don't have to enjoy every kind of sexual activity in order to be a sexually healthy person.* If some activity completely turns you off, not matter how much you think and talk about it, or how gingerly you try it, that's okay, as long as your feelings are not preventing you from freely expressing yourself in other sexual ways. Usually the more sexually hesitant person in a relationship feels a greater pressure to become less "inhibited." When there are many discrepancies between partners in their desires for sexual activities, problems may result. But if there are just a few areas of mismatched tastes, and there usually are a few for most couples, mutual consideration and respect seem to work best.

Perhaps the most important thing to remember is to try to change those areas that seem to be changeable and important to both of you, and not to blame yourself or resent your partner for not being able to get past his/her discomfort. Keep in mind that attitudes and interests sometimes evolve slowly, and you may find it amazingly easy to try an activity next year that you would not think of trying now.

Even in the best of relationships, suggesting something new

to do sexually can feel like a risky experience. "Will he/she think that our sex is terrible or dull because I want to try something different?" Both partners need to feel like *they* won't be rejected (even though a particular idea might be), and that at least they can feel free enough to bring something up to be talked about. This goes back to our earlier discussion of the general support and trust that are necessary when someone initiates and when someone chooses to refuse a sexual activity.

ORAL-GENITAL AND ANAL LOVEMAKING

But what about specifics? One way to enhance sexual relationships is to explore *oral-genital sex*. When done to the female, oral-genital sex is called *cunnilingus,* when done to the male it is called *fellatio.*

A freqent concern of both men and women about oral-genital activity is cleanliness. We have mentioned how most of us grow up with the idea that the genital area is dirty. Even though you may now realize that genitals are as clean as any other parts of your body, you may still feel uncomfortable about touching them with your mouth.

One way that we have found helps couples to deal with this concern is to take a shower together and to spend some time washing each other's genitals. This not only helps assure clean and fresh smelling genitals, but gently lathering the genital area with soap and warm water can provide a lot of sensual pleasure.

Another worry that couples often have is exactly how to provide good oral stimulation to their partner. If this is true for you, let your partner guide you with some suggestions on what feels best. One pattern that you might try is to begin with fondling genitals and gently nuzzling *around* the genitals—the stomach, thighs, and pubic hair. During fellatio, the woman can hold the penis and take the tip of it into her mouth, or run her tongue around the coronal ridge of her partner's penis. The coronal area, especially on the underneath side of the penis (the side closest to the scrotum) is especially sensitive. It's important that the woman do only as much stimulation as she feels comfortable providing. At first, a little genital touching and kissing may be the extent of fellatio. Later, perhaps after many experiences like this, she may feel comfortable providing more direct stimulation to the penis. At this time, try varying the pressure and rhythm on the penis. Many women find it difficult to encompass the length of the erect penis in their mouth. It is not necessary to move your mouth back and forth over the entire length in order to provide good stimulation; instead you might try using your hand to stimulate the lower part of the penis (near his body) and your mouth in a similar rhythm across the upper part of the penis. A good way to discover the best tempo is to follow your partner's movements and responses.

During oral stimulation to the woman, the same progression can be used. Begin slowly and gradually around the genitals, and then provide more direct stimulation to the clitoral area. Some women like very slow tongue movements, others like a very rapid flicking movement across the clitoris, or a sucking motion applied to the clitoris. Start slowly, and build tempo and pressure according to what the particular woman enjoys. Some communication is helpful. It's important that you *both* enjoy what is going on. One cautionary note: Although oral stimulation to the vagina is a pleasurable source of stimulation for women, the male should never blow air into the vagina, since air can enter the blood stream directly and be extremely dangerous to her health.

During oral stimulation, many couples enjoy touching other areas of the body at the same time. The male might fondle the woman's breasts or thighs while stimulating her genitals: the woman might stroke her partner's scrotal area during fellatio. Sometimes touching or holding a part of your partner's body while he/she is orally stimulating you is a nice way to feel closer and more mutually involved.

There are several different positions in which oral-genital stimulation is possible. The one who is being stimulated can stand with their partner kneeling or sitting, lie down with their partner lying down between their legs, or sit on the edge of a bed or comfortable chair with their partner kneeling before them. Another position couples use is for the one being stimulated to sit on the upper chest of their partner who is lying down. In this position, the partner who is being stimulated is almost kneeling above the other's face. The one who is doing the pleasuring is free to fondle the other partner's breasts or testicles; or if the female is being stimulated, she can manually stimulate her partner's penis. Try experimenting to find which positions are favorites for you.

Oral-genital stimulation does not always have to result in orgasm. It can be used during foreplay to pleasure each other. It can last just a short while before or after intercourse, or you can continue it for as long as you like. As we discussed earlier, many women (and men) do not like the idea of ejaculating into the woman's mouth. If this is true for you, you should work out some convenient signal so this doesn't happen.

On the other hand, you may prefer to allow the male to go ahead and ejaculate inside the woman's mouth. Some women do not find the taste or consistency of this fluid unpleasant and usually swallow it. Of course, there is no danger of becoming pregnant, and doing this is not harmful in any way. However, if the woman does not wish to swallow the ejaculate, it is possible to learn to position her mouth in such a way that when the man ejaculates, she merely holds the fluid in her mouth and afterwards rinses it out or disposes of it into a tissue. As a couple, you need to work out a pattern that is mutually satisfying to both of you.

Mutual oral-genital stimulation, commonly called "sixty-nine," is something you might want to try if you are both comfortable with fellatio and cunnilingus. Although many couples enjoy mutual stimulation, it is sometimes difficult to enjoy giving and receiving oral pleasure at the same time. Positions can also be a problem, and you will have to experiment to find one that suits you best. Having the woman on top allows her to better control the depth of the penis, although this is also possible with a side-to-side position.

Anal stimulation is also very arousing for some couples. You can manually stimulate this area during intercourse or foreplay. If you do try anal intercourse (inserting the penis into the anus), it's important to proceed very slowly and gradually. The anal muscles are much tighter than the vaginal muscles, and physical damage plus a good deal of pain may result if this is done too roughly. A lubricant such as K–Y jelly is necessary and a comfortable position to use is with the woman lying on her back with her legs slightly bent at the knees, and her hands free to guide her partner if necessary. Some couples like to use pillows under the woman's buttocks as well. If you have never tried anal intercourse, it is best to start out with inserting a finger, slowly and gently. Over several sessions, you should be able to insert two fingers. It is especially important to make certain that the woman is not experiencing any discomfort. One way to insure this is to let the woman guide the man as to how fast and how hard to thrust. If any discomfort does occur, try again some other time.

After the woman has become used to the insertion of two fingers, you can try penile stimulation. Again, go slowly— trying one, two, or three fingers first before trying to insert the penis. Make sure that the penis is well lubricated the K–Y or a lubricated condom.

It's very important that you *not* go on to vaginal intercourse immediately after you have tried anal intercourse. The reason for this is that some of the natural bacteria in the rectum may cause vaginal infections if they are transmitted from the anus to the vagina. If you do want to have vaginal intercourse right after anal intercourse, the man should wear a condom during anal intercourse and then remove it before going on to vaginal stimulation; or if anal intercourse without a condom takes place, the man should wash his penis well with soap and water before going on.

OTHER FORMS OF ENHANCEMENT

There are as many variations to sexual activity as you care to take advantage of—enhancement depends upon you and your partner. You can try having sex at a different time of the day, waking up your partner during the night, or finding a private place out of doors. If you usually like to be freshly showered for sex, you might try making love after some sweaty activity on a warm summer day. Or, if you generally like to spend a long time making love, try a "quickie"—some frantic lovemaking before you have to be somewhere. Try to think of ways that would expand *your* particular sexual experiences. Some books, like Alex Comfort's *Joy of Sex,* will give you some basic ideas from which to begin.

From time to time, newspapers or magazines mention aphrodisiacs—various substances that might increase sexual desire. Alcohol is often thought to increase sexual desire by decreasing a person's inhibitions. In small amounts, alcohol does tend to relax people, which may or may not make sexual arousal easier. In larger amounts, alcohol has a negative effect on sexual desire, and frequently it can interfere with the male's ability to have or to maintain an erection.

Marijuana may also act to decrease inhibitions, but it does not necessarily act as a sexual stimulant. Some people report feeling more sexual pleasure and others report less sexual pleasure after smoking marijuana. Other drugs such as amphetamines, amyl nitrate ("poppers") and cantharides ("Spanish fly") may cause temporary increases in sexual desire, but they all can have dangerous, and even lethal, side effects. Poppers and Spanish fly cause dilation of the blood vessels, with the latter also causing severe inflammation of the urinary tract.

Perhaps the best physical aphrodisiacs are feeling healthy and being physically active. This helps you to feel better about yourself and more energetic. If your physical condition concerns you and you would like to make some changes along these lines, there are some books in the Bibliography that will give you a start.

DELAYING EJACULATION

Increasing the pleasure you get from sex often involves giving yourselves more time for a relaxed sensuous experience. Often, however, what a couple does sexually is determined by when the male partner ejaculates. Orgasm does not have to be the goal of lovemaking, and it does not have to signal the end of a sexual encounter. Although at times you may want to continue pleasuring after the male has ejaculated, you may also, at times, desire to delay ejaculation for a while. It is possible to do this through techniques which seem to inhibit this reflex. Originally, a technique was developed by Dr. James Semans in 1959 in order to teach men to extend the time to ejaculation. Later, the Seman's procedure was modified by Masters and Johnson and has become known as the "squeeze" technique.

The idea behind both techniques (the pause and the squeeze) is that the man learns to control the timing of ejaculation without decreasing the amount of stimulation or the erotic pleasure of arousal and orgasm. He learns to delay ejaculation either by pausing and stopping all sexual stimulation or by squeezing on a certain place on the penis.

It's important for the male to learn to determine when he's going to ejaculate. Most men are aware of a special sensation which signals that ejaculation is about to occur. This is sometimes called the feeling of "inevitability," because the reflex has been triggered and will occur automatically whether or not stimulation is continued. This response seems to be unique to men; among women, discontinuing stimulation will almost always prevent orgasm from occurring.

Pausing: If the pause technique is used, stimulation and movement must stop just *before* the feeling of inevitability occurs. The male then waits until his high level of arousal subsides and he feels that stimulation can be resumed. Some men will experience a partial loss of erection, but renewed stimulation will bring this back. The advantage to the pause technique is that it is relatively simple. If the pause is used during intercourse, the man doesn't need to withdraw but can simply stop all movement. Couples often enjoy using these brief moments to experience feelings of closeness and gentle caressing.

A possible disadvantage is that pauses during intercourse may interfere with the woman's buildup of arousal and her orgasmic response. One way to deal with this would be for the man to stimulate his partner manually until movement can be resumed.

It's important that the male receive a lot of stimulation rather than a little. This will allow him to get accustomed to prolonged arousal without interfering with the enjoyment of sexual stimulation. We also suggest that the male partner *not* try to control his ejaculation by thinking about something else (work, an unpleasant scene, etc.)—not only does this work poorly, but it also decreases the pleasurable erotic quality of the sexual experience. The pause technique takes practice—probably several weeks—but the more it is used, the more effective it will become. For this reason, the male may choose to practice ejaculatory control on his own. This can be done by masturbating and using the pause two or three times a week. Usually the man will find that after a while he can continue 10 to 15 minutes of active stimulation with between zero and three pauses. These individual masturbation sessions are helpful for a number of reasons.

1. They allow for practice in learning when to pause. It's useful to learn when is too late as well as too early to pause. There will be times when this is misjudged and ejaculation happens anyway. Don't worry if this situation does occur; missing the moment is another way of learning to better identify it the next time.

2. The man is free to experiment with varying the length of time he pauses. It's important to learn how long the pause needs to be in order to allow stimulation to be continued for another period of time. At first, the male may find he needs to pause up to five minutes. After practice, the pause may be down to one minute or less. Keeping a written record is often helpful in order to see the progression of shorter pauses, fewer pauses, and increasing amounts of sexual stimulation. Of course, control during masturbation is likely to be a lot easier than control during foreplay or intercourse. It's a good idea to use lubricant, fantasy, and erotic material such as pictures or stories during masturbation to help the physical experience seem more stimulating.

The Squeeze: The squeeze technique is an alternative that some couples prefer. During the squeeze procedure, the man or the woman applies pressure to a certain area on the penis just before the moment at which ejaculation seems inevitable. This will inhibit the ejaculatory reflex and enable the couple to resume sexual stimulation. Often, the man will lose some of his erection until stimulation is resumed.

The squeeze can be applied either by the male or the female, and, like the pause, practice improves control. Probably the best way to begin learning this skill is for the man to use the squeeze during masturbation. He can then experiment with when to squeeze, and with how hard and how long to squeeze. The squeeze involves using the thumb and next two fingers. The thumb is placed just under the coronal ridge with the other two fingers directly opposite on the other side of the penile shaft.

Sufficient pressure must be applied to stop ejaculation. Often men (and more often women!) are surprised at the amount of pressure which can be applied to the erect penis without causing discomfort. This is because the erect penis is filled with blood and because it contains a lot of spongy tissue which helps absorb the pressure that is applied.

Some men find that positioning their fingers in the way we've described does not lessen their arousal level but rather triggers ejaculation. This is usually because a) the man continued stimulation too long, and ejaculation had already begun; or b) the position of the fingers on the head of the penis creates extra stimulation. If this happens, try applying the squeeze just under the coronal ridge, without touching the head of the penis.

If the squeeze is practiced during masturbation, the man should provide plenty of vigorous stimulation before squeezing. Often, fantasy or the use of erotic material such as pictures or stories help increase arousal and the sexual quality of the experience. As with the pause, over time, the man will probably be able to engage in 15 minutes of stimulation with zero to three squeezes, and the length of time he needs to squeeze should become briefer and briefer.

Practicing these techniques during masturbation is not absolutely necessary if strong feelings about masturbation make this difficult. However, we would encourage men to re-evaluate any negative feelings in light of the benefits to be gained. Possibly some of the ideas expressed in Chapter 3 will be useful. Should you still decide to practice these techniques not using masturbation, it will, as we said earlier, be important to be patient and cooperate in finding the best mutually acceptable way to gradually learn to control ejaculation.

AGING AND SEXUALITY

You may be surprised to find a discussion on sex and aging in a chapter on enhancement. Often, however, the changes that take place in the sexual cycle of older men and women enable a couple to explore new avenues of sensual pleasure. A book that deals in some detail with these changes is *Sound Sex and The Aging Heart,* by Lee D. Scheingold and Nathaniel N. Wagner (see Bibliography).

There are some obvious changes that both men and women will notice as they grow older. It will take longer for the man to achieve an erection and for the woman to begin lubricating. There may also be less total lubrication produced. The older male has greater ejaculatory control and can maintain an erection for a longer period than a younger man. However, the feeling of "inevitability" which signals ejaculation is often not experienced by the older male. Occasionally ejaculation will not occur at all.

After orgasm, the physical changes that have occurred during sexual arousal will return very rapidly to the unaroused state—this is true for both men and women.

Knowing what to expect as your body ages enables you to take advantage of some of these natural changes. For example, since it usually takes longer for erection to occur in older men, foreplay often becomes a more relaxed, sensuous experience for many couples. Also, the longer time to ejaculation allows for extended foreplay and longer intercourse, an experience that may have previously been rare or nonexistent.

The fact that the older male may not ejaculate during sex often causes great concern. Unless a couple accepts this as a normal aspect of aging in the male, they are likely to experience anxiety and frustration in their attempts for orgasm. Sometimes, switching stimulation—for example, from intercourse to oral-genital or manual pleasuring—will enable the male to ejaculate. At other times, however, a feeling of pleasure and enjoyment from sexual closeness is possible even though ejaculation does not occur.

Other changes, both physical and emotional, add to the enhancement of sex in later life. Skin texture often changes, becoming softer and smoother, and feelings of trust and comfortableness between partners in a long-term relationship add to the enjoyment of sex. For many couples, menopause, which signals the end of the woman's child-bearing years, often means a new freedom from worries about contraception and allows sexual expression to become more spontaneous.

For the older female, intercourse may bring some discomfort because of a normal thinning of the lining of the vaginal walls. This can be eliminated, however, through the use of lubricating creams and/or hormone treatments.

Although changes do occur, sexual responsiveness and the desire for sex do not disappear with age. Studies have shown that men and women often continue to be sexually active through and beyond their 70s. Two important factors in continuing sexual interest and functioning seem to be a fairly active sex life with regular sexual contact, and the availability of a sexual partner. Rather than indicate the end of sexuality, aging permits expansion, enhancement, and continued sexual growth.

CONCLUSION

There are many other areas of sexuality that we have not considered here which are important. Premarital and extramarital sex, the problems of sexual partners for divorced or widowed women, the value of homosexual relationships, and many other facets of sexual expression are topics that deserve a good deal of special consideration. The unique problems and emotions in these areas go beyond what we can adequately deal with in one short book. We suggest that if you are interested in, or living in any of these situations, you check the Bibliography for books that deal with these specific areas. We hope that the basic ideas and feelings we've discussed in the previous chapters with regard to the development of your own sexuality with and without a partner is a good beginning for you, whatever your particular set of circumstances at the present moment.

12

What Next?

It may be that you will still be dissatisfied with your own sexuality or your sexual relationship with your partner after following the program in this book. If this turns out to be the case for you, the logical question is, what to do next.

There are a number of approaches you might consider. First, try to specify exactly what it is that you are dissatisfied about. Are your concerns reasonable, in the light of what you have learned about female sexuality and the couple relationship? Or are you aiming for unrealistic goals? The most obvious realistic concern would be if you have not had an orgasm, either by yourself or with your partner, by this time. Some unrealistic concerns are a wish to have an orgasm during intercourse every time, to always have simultaneous orgasms with your partner, or to be multiply orgasmic. Although all of these goals may be things you would like to experience at some point, it is perhaps a little too much to expect them right now. Remember, you have been making some big changes in yourself and your sexuality as you followed this program; and it may take some time for these changes to stabilize and make further growth possible.

If, however, you do feel dissatisfied with the results of this program, or if you are reasonably happy with the results so far but would like to make further gains, there are a variety of approaches to consider. You should think over each of the following alternatives carefully, and discuss them with your partner, if you have one. Which alternative fits best for your current concern, and which approach is likely to be productive for you, are judgments that only you can make. Some alternatives:

Let nature take its course. If you have attained your most immediate goals, but still feel you would like to continue to grow, you might consider just relaxing and enjoying your new sexuality at this point. As you continue to have pleasurable self and/or partner sessions, you will more or less automatically find that your attitudes continue to become more positive: Your sexual arousal will increase, you will gain skill at arousing yourself, and your orgasmic capacity will grow. Additionally, as you and your partner continue to learn about each other and to communicate with each other, sex between the two of you will also become more pleasurable. This process is one we have seen in our patients after we finish active therapy with them. By follow-up time (three to six months after the end of therapy), most women (and couples) report further growth.

Do some more work on your own. If you have not reached some of your important goals, but feel that you are changing and that you have seen some progress during this program, you (and your partner) may want to continue to work on your own. If there are specific areas of your own sexuality or your relationship that concern you, you may want to re-read the relevant sections of this book, and repeat the prescribed exercises. A "second try" often produces results where the first attempt did not.

Additionally, you may want to read some other books that can be helpful. A bibliography is included at the end of this book as a guide. The Bibliography has a brief note on what each book is about, to help you in picking out the most relevant book for your particular concerns.

There are other sources of additional information that may also be helpful to you. Does your local college or adult education program have courses on sexuality, marriage, personal health, exercise, and so forth that would benefit you? Does your local church, woman's club, or other community organization sponsor lectures, workshops, or "retreats" on these topics? Are there "X rated" movie theatres or adult bookstores near you that can provide some additional fantasy material? You may be surprised to discover just how much is available if you start pursuing these different sources of new information.

Work with a therapist. This option is one you may consider if this program has not really produced any significant results for you. You may feel that you want individual therapy for your own personal concerns (such as self-esteem, moods, etc.) marital or relationship therapy if your general relationship with your partner is troubling you, or specific "sex therapy" if your primary concern is your sexuality or sexual relationship with your partner. Again, you must think, discuss, and decide which of these modes of therapy is most likely to meet your needs now.

Whichever mode of therapy you choose, you will next be faced with the difficult process of choosing a therapist. There are two major components in making this choice, and unfortunately, there are no clear cut, easy rules for making such a decision.

The first issue in making your choice concerns the competence of the therapist. Psychotherapy is offered by a number of different professional specialists—psychologists, psychiatrists, social workers, and pastoral counselors, to name just a few. It's important that you have a lot of information about any therapist's training, qualifications, and ability. In lieu of direct information access to a therapist's qualifications, you may want to concentrate your selection upon the clinical psychologists or psychiatrists in your area. The reason for this is that both the professional training and the state licensing or certification laws are more rigorous for these disciplines than for the others. This is not to say that all other specialists are not competent (or that all psychologists and psychiatrists *are* competent); but in the absence of direct knowledge of a particular therapist's ability, this rule is a helpful "first screening" of possible alterantives.

In choosing a clinical psychologist or psychiatrist, be sure that he or she is licensed as such in your state. This insures that the therapist is formally qualified, by training and experience, to conduct psychotherapy. Additionally, certification by either the American Board of Psychiatry and Neurology or the American Board of Professional Psychology, over and above state licensure or certification, provides another safeguard for you. Don't be embarrassed to ask about these certifications and licensures. No responsible professional is anything but pleased to work with a client who has reassured herself about the therapist's formal qualifications.

As a next step in insuring therapist competence, you might try to get some personal opinions about your prospective therapists. While therapists do not provide letters of reference from satisfied customers, such information can often be found. Your family doctor, minister, and, again, friends can often recommend a therapist on the basis of direct personal knowledge of the therapist's ability.

How does one locate a therapist? There are a number of alternatives. Your county Medical Society can provide you with the names of psychiatrists, and your County or State Psychological Association can provide a list of licensed clinical psychologists. If you live near a university or medical school, try contacting the Department of Psychiatry and/or Psychology. Training programs in psychiatry and clinical psychology usually run an outpatient clinic where you can obtain qualified therapy, often at a reduced fee compared to private practitioners. If there is a city, county, or state mental health clinic near you, you may also contact their outpatient clinic for therapy or a referral.

Once you have located some therapists who meet the qualifications discussed above, you must then make a second and more difficult choice: Among several qualified therapists, which one is likely to be best *for you*?

As a first step in making this decision, try to match the therapist's specialty with your concern. If you are concerned about *yourself*, seek out someone who does primarily individual psychotherapy. If your *relationship* concerns you, seek out someone who specializes in marital therapy. We recommend that you find a clinical psychologist or psychiatrist who meets the criteria listed above and who specializes in marriage, rather than going to a "marriage counselor" or "marriage therapist." The reason for this is that state laws vary—in some states, literally anyone can represent themselves as a "marriage counselor."

A similar situation exists in regard to "sex therapy." If your concerns are primarily sexual, seek out a licensed and certified clinical psychologist or psychiatrist who has had additional training in sex therapy and now specializes in this area. We do not recommend that you go to a "sex therapist" because again, there are no state licensure laws to regulate who can use that "title," and indeed there is no such professional discipline to insure adequate training of such people. Once again, your county Medical Society, State Psychological Association, or department of Psychology or Psychiatry at the nearest university or medical school should be able to provide the name of someone who specializes in sexual therapy.

Having found a therapist who is formally qualified and who specializes in your area of concern, the decision about *this* therapist's ability to help you now becomes a personal matter. Therapists differ in their theoretical orientation, of course, and while there is no clear cut evidence that any one particular approach is more effective than another, some types of therapy work best for particular problems and for particular types of people. Decide what you want out of therapy, and have a frank and open discussion with your prospective therapist in the first session. Does he or she agree that your goals are reasonable? Ask for a brief description of the type of therapy he or she conducts: Does it seem to get at your concerns? If not, discuss with the therapist what you would like to work on, and how. The therapist may convince you to try things in a different way than you had originally planned, which can be quite valid. Alternatively, the therapist may provide you with a referral to a colleague who is a better match for your expectations. Once in therapy with someone, realize that therapy is a difficult and demanding process. Don't quit early, or "doctor-shop"—don't jump from therapist to therapist looking for someone who will "cure" you *without any effort* or difficulty on your part. At the same time, if you are dissatisfied with your therapy, discuss this with the therapist rather than just quitting. You may decide that this therapist is not for you; but talk about this with the therapist and mutually decide what to do (continue, quit, referral to another therapist) rather than just dropping out.

If you do feel a need for further growth, do pursue one of these pathways to additional change. With the passage of time, further work on your own, or psychotherapy, you can make progress. Everyone has the capacity for change and growth, and only your own refusal to try can prevent you from growing and changing.

Overview

CHAPTER 2 GETTING TO KNOW YOURSELF

1. Your personal sex history.
2. Visual exploration of your body—one or two sessions 45 minutes to one hour.

CHAPTER 3 EXPLORATION BY TOUCH

1. Sessions of at least 30 minutes to one hour each.
2. Try deep muscle relaxation, and body awareness exercises at least three to five times a week until you can relax yourself fairly easily. Muscle control exercise is optional. Continue using throughout the program either before sessions or at other times of the day to relax.

3. Kegel vaginal exercises. Do each 10 times twice a day for the first week; 10 times each twice a day for the rest of the program.

CHAPTER 4 TOUCHING FOR PLEASURE: DISCOVERY

1. Have at least two sessions at least 15–30 minutes each.

CHAPTER 5 TOUCHING FOR PLEASURE: FOCUSING

1. About three times a week for one or two weeks, 30–45 minutes each time.
2. Do loosening exercises and sensate focus at least twice and try either exercise, but especially sensate focus prior to your sessions.
3. Try fantasy and/or erotic literature prior to or during sessions.
4. Continue using relaxation, fantasy, erotica, loosening or sensate focus as you find them helpful to more easily become involved in your self pleasuring sessions.

CHAPTER 6 BECOMING MORE INVOLVED

1. At least four self-pleasuring sessions.
2. Role-play orgasm—two-three times early in self pleasuring sessions. Try orgasm triggers as you become aroused. Pleasuring sessions should last 20 minutes to one hour.
3. Continue to use orgasm triggers during high arousal, if they seem to help maintain or increase feelings of pleasure.

CHAPTER 7 USING A VIBRATOR: A LITTLE HELP FROM A FRIEND

1. Use vibrator for general body massage, at least twice for 15–30 minutes.

2. As vibrator stimulation of genitals is included, extend sessions to 45 minutes for at least five to six different sessions.

CHAPTER 8 SHARING SELF DISCOVERIES WITH YOUR PARTNER

1. Sharing masturbation with your partner is optional. Read entire chapter before deciding if you want to move on to Chapter 9. If you decide to do this, try once or twice, taking as much time (at least 30 minutes) as you both need to feel comfortable.
2. Role-play initiation and refusal.
3. Whatever was pleasurable or arousing during self sessions should be continued through couple experiences; for example, fantasy, vibrator, orgasm triggers.

CHAPTER 9 PLEASURING EACH OTHER

1. Spend an hour or more over three to six sessions until you both feel more comfortable. Make use of verbal and non-verbal communication.
2. Explore the use of the vibrator together on one or two sessions (optional depending on the woman's needs or the couple's preferences).

CHAPTER 10 INTERCOURSE: ANOTHER FORM OF MUTUAL PLEASURING

1. At least four to five sessions of 40 minutes or more to explore positions for pleasurable stimulation.
2. Couple sessions should become flexible to sometimes alternate non-intercourse with intercourse sessions.

Note to Professionals

Much of our work with women in therapy has been in context of short term, dual-sex therapy teams that focus on the woman but include her sexual partner as well. However, the program outlined in this book has also been successful for women without partners in individual and group therapy. Details of our therapy approach are discussed in a cassette tape entitled "Behavioral Treatment of Sexual Dysfunction" by Joseph LoPiccolo, which is available from Biomonitoring Applications, 270 Madison Avenue, New York, New York 10016.

Briefly, we would like to mention how several different therapeutic approaches might make use both of this program and three 15 minute films that are specifically designed to enhance the ease of trying each step. The films are entitled: *Becoming Orgasmic: A Sexual Growth Program for Women,* and are available from Focus International, Inc., 505 West End Avenue, New York,

New York. The first two films, subtitled "Discovery" and "Self-Pleasuring," can be used for women with or without a current sexual partner, thus complementing the material in Chapters 2–7. The final film, "Sharing", is for women who do have a sexual partner, and it follows the content of Chapter 8–10. All three films show one woman's exploration of her body, the pleasure it can provide for her, and her growing sexual response through orgasm. Some of the common reactions, doubts, and uncertainties that accompany each stage of growth are also expressed. We feel that the films are useful as models for overcoming some of the uncertainties of progressing through the program. The films may be of particular benefit to male therapists since they provide a female model who self-discloses her fears and concerns.

If a Woman is Involved in Individual or Couple Therapy. The actual exercises are outlined clearly in the preceding chapters. Although some discussion of them may be necessary, more therapy time should probably be spent on the particular woman's feelings about each step, both before and after she tries to do them. We recommend that the therapist have the woman write down her reactions to each exercise (What was difficult? easy? How did she feel? How pleasurable was it?) as soon as possible after each attempt to do a specific part. These written records should be brought to the therapy session. We have found that they are efficient and effective means to understanding any difficulties the woman may be having. The questions presented within the chapters themselves might form an additional basis for discussion.

If the films are also used, the therapist might show each step before a woman tries it herself. A preliminary view of the film would be particularly useful to explain how to go about each exercise, or at those points that seem particularly emotion-laden for the individual woman. It would allow a chance for her to react and to ask questions. However, some parts of the film may be better used after the woman has tried on her own, in case she might tend to form a particular set on how she should respond. The decision on when to show the films should be based on the material involved and on the particular woman's strengths and sensitivities.

If the Woman is Involved in Group Therapy. Small groups of women may also use the book and films in a format similar to that for individual or couple therapy. Group therapy also provides a unique opportunity for women to gain perspectives on their sexual growth; and when handled well, a group can offer additional support beyond the individual therapy experience. Care should be taken in forming a group—one of the most important variables is that of a current sexual partner. Groups seem to work better if they are homogeneous as to whether or not the women are involved in a permanent, long term relationship with someone. Additionally, it may be helpful to separate those women who have never had orgasm from those who are infrequently orgasmic.

In any case, it is important for the therapist to encourage mutual support among the group members, and discourage any tendencies for comparison among the different rates of progress that will occur. To focus early on the expectation that each woman has an individualized rate of progress should be a useful beginning.

For those women who do have sexual partners, the third film and Chapters 8–10 are intended for the couple to use together. Although the partner's participation in the group may be extremely helpful, it is not a requirement. It is possible for the woman to transmit the information she has gained to her partner on her own, as long as they have a very good and cooperative relationship. If the partner does want to be part of the actual therapy, he can be included in several ways. One possibility is to have part of each of the later group sessions include the male partners. Another possibility is to have an additional meeting set aside for the males only, with less time spent in a combined male-female sessions.

Regardless of the therapeutic format, there are a few guiding principles that are important to keep in mind. First, the woman should be aware that learning to have an orgasm is only one part of sexual growth, and that it will involve more than just learning a series of techniques. Second, the woman's personal feelings and thoughts are extremely important to the ease or difficulty she may have at various points. Feelings should not be seen as secondary to the actual "doing" of the various steps. Third, orgasm is likely to be different from what the woman expected; and some time should be spent discussing how it differs from expectations and what that difference means to her. Fourth, as women become more sexually responsive, those who have permanent partners may find some uncertainty on the male's part in accepting her changes. Time should be spent both with the woman and her partner to deal with any covert or overt problems that may accompany the woman's sexual growth.

A Selected Annotated Bibliography

The following books discuss a variety of aspects of personal and sexual growth. They vary in style from very personal information sharing to more technical academic presentations. Obviously the list is a selective one and we view it as a good starting point. The starred(*) titles are for those readers who want only a representative selection from a particular category.

GENERAL SEX INFORMATION

This group of books offers an overview of general information on sexual behavior, sexual attitudes, and the treatment of male and female sexual problems.

*Katchadourian, H. A. and Lunde D. T. *Fundamentals of Human Sexuality.* New York: Holt, Rinehart & Winston, 1975.

McCary, J. L. *Human Sexuality.* New York: Van Nostrand, 1973. These are basic texts used in college and undergraduate courses; they include a study of the full range of sexual behavior.

McCary, J. L. *Sexual Myths and Fallacies.* New York: Van Nostrand, 1971. Good overview of sexual myths and clarification of facts regarding each area of misinformation.

Brecher, R. and Brecher, E. *An Analysis of Human Sexual Response.* New York: Bantam, 1966. A good readable summary of Masters and Johnson's laboratory research on sexual response. Also contains other papers on human sexuality.

*Lehrman, N. *Masters and Johnson Explained.* Chicago: Playboy Press, 1970. A readable discussion of the Masters and Johnson work, with primary emphasis on how they treat sexual dysfunctions. Also contains an interview with Masters and Johnson.

Robbins, J. and Robbins, J. *An Analysis of Human Sexual Inadequacy.* New York: Signet, 1970. Contains a discussion of Masters and Johnson's treatment program plus other articles on various aspects of sexuality.

Hunt, M. *Sexual Behavior in the 1970s.* Chicago: Playboy Press, 1974. A recent survey of a limited sample of Americans that suggests some trends in sexual standards on premarital sex, extramarital relations, and homosexuality.

Ford, C. F. and Beech, F. A. *Patterns of Sexual Behavior.* New York: Harper & Row, 1970 (Original Edition 1951). Substantial cross-cultural and cross-species summary of studies on sexual behavior. Dated material, but well integrated and accurate.

*Morrison, E. S. and Borosage, V. *Human Sexuality: Contemporary Perspectives.* Palo Alto: National Press Books, 1973. A nice selection of readings on sexual development, sex roles, marriage and extramarital affairs, pornography and homosexuality.

II. BODYWORK

Books on relaxation, massage, and other topics dealing with ways to use, improve, and enjoy your body.

*Downing, G. *The Massage Book.* New York: Random House, 1972. Illustrated, complete guide to massage, including couple and self-massage and mention of meditation techniques.

Inkeles, G. and Todris, M. *The Art of Sensual Massage.* San Francisco: Straight Arrow Books, 1972. Illustrated. Emphasizes the use of touch as a form of communication and as a way to achieve sensual pleasure.

Whelan, S. and Cochran, R. *The Art of Erotic Massage.* New York: A Signet Book, The New American Library, Inc., 1972. Illustrates different massage techniques and their use in creating sensual and sexual pleasure.

Young, C. *Self-Massage.* New York: A Bantam Minibook, Bantam Books, Inc., 1973. Techniques for relaxation and renewal through self-massage.

Rosenberg, J. *Total Orgasm.* New York: Random House, 1973. Exercises for men and women to enhance sexual responsiveness.

*Ubell, E. *How to Save Your Life.* Harcourt, Brace, Jovanovich, Inc., New York: 1973, How to modify your life style to live longer and with better health. Discusses work pressures, smoking, drinking, overeating, and sex.

Scheingold, L. D. and Wagner, N. N. *Sound Sex and the Aging Heart.* New York: Behavioral Publications, 1974. Discusses sex and aging with special reference to people with cardiac problems.

Cooper, K. H. *The New Aerobics.* New York: Bantam, 1970. A useful individual exercise guide designed to develop general and cardiovascular functioning and help maintain it throughout life.

Bowerman, W. J. and Harris, W. E. *Jogging—A Medically Approved Physical Fitness Program For All Ages.* New York: Grosset and Dunlap, 1967. A medically sound program for developing fitness. Progress geared to individual levels, gradually increasing stamina.

Stuart, R. B. and Davis, B. *Slim Chance in a Fat World.* Condensed version. Champagne, Illinois: Research Press, 1972. A sensible weight reduction program that concentrates on changing eating patterns rather than just cutting calories.

III. RELIGION AND SEXUALITY

The books in this section deal with sexuality in relation to morality and Christianity. Unfortunately, we are not aware of any comparable popular books confronting issues on Judaism and sexuality.

*Steinmetz, U. G. *The Sexual Christian.* St. Meinrad, Indiana: Abbey Press, 1972. Discusses the man/woman relationship, marriage, and sexuality. Proposes that anti-sexual prohibitions are not a true part of Christian thought.

Bird, J. and Bird, L. *The Freedom of Sexual Love.* New York: Doubleday, 1970. For Catholics. Carries the Nihil Obstat and Imprimatur, indicating that the book is "free of doctrinal or moral error." Contains material helpful for those with religious concerns about sexuality.

IV. PERSONAL GROWTH

The following books address areas of self-esteem, confidence, and personal awareness. All of them make specific suggestions on how to go about understanding where you are and how to change.

*Rush, A. K. *Getting Clear.* New York: Random House, 1973. A book for women on becoming more aware of yourself physically, emotionally, and intellectually. Written in a warm, personal style with numerous exercises. Topics covered include: body awareness, massage, sex roles, communication, abortion, childbirth, meditation, consciousness raising.

*The Boston Women's Health Collective. *Our Bodies, Our Selves.* New York: Simon & Schuster, 1973. Very informative book about the experience of being a woman. Includes anatomy and physiology, sexuality, relationships, lesbianism, rape, nutrition, birth control, pregnancy, menopause and self-help health care.

Bach, G. R. and Wyden, P. *The Intimate Enemy.* New York: Avon, 1968. For those women with partners, this book discusses the value of fighting and how to benefit from fighting in constructive ways. Discusses problems of intimacy.

Ellis, A. and Harper, R. A. *A New Guide to Rational Living.* North Hollywood, Calif.: Wilshire Book Company, 1975. A book that helps you develop a rational approach to dealing with problems.

O'Neill, N. and O'Neill, G. *Shifting Gears.* New York: Avon Books, 1974. Deals with life crises usually associated with the middle years. For instance: divorce, death, loss of job, changing life styles.

V. OTHER SEXUAL GROWTH BOOKS

These books are more personal than the books listed above under General Sex Information or Personal Growth. As such, they may be useful for further growth in attitude change, sexual technique, and so forth.

Barbach, L. G. *For Yourself.* New York: Doubleday, 1975. A description of a group therapy program for inorgasmic women.

McCarthy, B. W., Ryan, M., and Johnson, F. A. *Sexual Awareness.* San Francisco, Calif.: Boyd and Fraser, 1975. A self-help program to enhance "self-awareness and pleasure giving."

*Hastings, D. W. *Sexual Expression in Marriage.* 2d ed. New York: Bantam, 1972. Covers both anatomy and physiology as well as sexual techniques, dysfunctions, and so forth.

Comfort, A. *The Joy of Sex.* New York: Crown, 1972.

Comfort, A. *More Joy.* New York: Crown, 1974. These best sellers are an "advanced course" in lovemaking techniques.

Dodson, B. *Liberating Masturbation.* New York: Bodysex Designs, 1974. A book on the benefits of masturbation and the use of the vibrator for women.

Ellis, A. *Sex Without Guilt.* New York: Lancer Books, 1966. Good for gaining a positive view of human sexuality.

VI. BOOKS FOR PROFESSIONALS

These books are recommended for therapists and other professionals who work with clients who have sexual problems or concerns.

Masters, W. H. and Johnson, V. E. *Human Sexual Response.* Boston: Little Brown, 1966. The classic work on the anatomy and physiology of sexual response cycle.

Masters, W. H. and Johnson, V. E. *Human Sexual Inadequacy.* Boston: Little Brown, 1970. Describes the basic treatment approach for sexual dysfunctions for males and females.

Kaplan, H. S. *The New Sex Therapy.* New York: Brunner/Mazel, 1974. Kaplan's therapy program adds some modifications to the Masters–Johnson format, including a discussion of psychoanalytic concepts in relation to sex therapy.

Kaplan, H. S. *The Illustrated Manual of Sex Therapy.* New York: Brunner/Mazel, 1975. A non-theoretical specific guide to the actual procedures and exercises used in sex therapy.

Annon, J. *The Behavioral Treatment of Sexual Problems.* Vol. I and Vol. II. Honolulu, Hawaii: Enabling Systems, 1974 and 1975. A description of the learning theory approach to sexual dysfunction, with many clinical examples.

Hartman, W. E. and Fithian, M. A. *Treatment of Sexual Dysfunction.* Long Beach, Calif.: Center for Marital and Sexual Studies,

1972. A non-traditional modification of the Masters and Johnson format.

Hastings, D. W. *Impotence and Frigidity.* Boston: Little, Brown, 1963. Describes many of the treatment programs for dysfunction.

Additionally, professionals who work in the area of sexuality may wish to subscribe to these professional journals:

Archives of Sexual Behavior (bimonthly), Plenum Publishing Co., New York.

Journal of Sex Research (quarterly), Society for Scientific Study of Sex, New York.

Two journal articles relevant to the particular program described in this book are:

LoPiccolo, J. and Lobitz, C. "The Role of Masturbation in the Treatment of Sexual Dysfunction." *Archives of Sexual Behavior* 2 (1972): 163–171.

Lobitz, C. and LoPiccolo, J. "New Methods in Behavioral Treatment of Sexual Dysfunction." *Journal of Behavior Therapy and Experimental Psychiatry* (1972): 3 (1972): 265–271.

Index

Wordsworth, *Lyrical Ballads* 1800

Achilles, *point of view on a journey* 138-39

Marge, *another literary meaning of* 15-17

novel, *multiple* 14